Acknowledged: The UFO Bombshell!

UFO Disclosure, Interdimensional Intelligence Discovered by The United States Government revealed in 2017

Table of Contents

Acknowledged: News	6
Acknowledged: 1960's	19
Acknowledged: 1970's	26
Acknowledged: White House	34
Acknowledged: The General	39
Acknowledged: NASA	41
Acknowledged: "The Others"	44
Acknowledged: Religion	52
Acknowledged: The 12 FACTS	63
Acknowledged: The Email	67
Acknowledged: Deaths of Investigators	69
Acknowledged: Bill Cooper	76
Acknowledged: DUMB Sites	92
Acknowledged: JPL & Crowley	114
Acknowledged: JPL & Aleister Crowley	97
Acknowledged: Antarctica	120
Acknowledged: Genesis	124

Fact

On April 9, 1983, investigative reporter Linda Moulton Howe was at Kirtland AFB in Albuquerque, New Mexico, interviewing an Air Force Office of Special Investigations Agent named Sgt. Richard C. Doty. During that meeting, Richard Doty handed her several typed pages as he said, "My superiors have asked me to show this to you. You can read the documents and ask me questions, but you can't take notes." The top page read in all capitols centered on the page:

**BRIEFING PAPER FOR THE
PRESIDENT OF THE UNITED STATES OF AMERICA
ON THE SUBJECT OF
UNIDENTIFIED AERIAL VEHICLES (UAVs)**

The paper summarized more than half a dozen crash retrievals of "extraterrestrial" aerial vehicles from a variety of locations in New Mexico and Arizona.
She then read a paragraph that said the Extraterrestrials had "manipulated DNA in an already evolving primate species to create homo sapiens."

Both Sgt. Richard C. Doty and Linda Moulton Howe have confirmed this meeting took place and agree about the content provided to Miss Howe.

Foreword

When you grow up in the United States with friends and relatives that have spent their lifetimes in the United States Air Force going back to World War Two you learn a lot of things that people without those contacts are shielded from. I've known about the reality of UFO's and things going on at Wright Patterson Airforce Base and other military facilities since the nineteen seventies. I've researched UFO's all my life.

What you are going to read in this book is the best available acknowledged evidence and testimony on the subject. Recently there have been incredible revelations made by a secret group of government insiders working with White House Chief of Staff Senior Presidential Advisor, John D. Podesta. The revelation is mind-blowing; the United States Government has identified an "interdimensional intelligence" that is responsible for not only the UFO phenomenon but also virtually all paranormal phenomenon experienced here on Earth.

For seventy years, behind the back of the American people there has been a multi trillion-dollar deep black budget effort within the Department of Defense and United States government contractors, aerospace corporations and research institutes trying to understand this phenomenon, communicate with entities beyond our understanding and trying to develop a military defense against forces beyond our understanding that have designs on our planet.

Underneath the surface of our nation, in deep underground military bases and secret facilities there exists another world filled with technology and realities unimaginable to the average citizen. The locations of over one hundred of these "DUMB" facilities are just some of what you will find in this book.

Don't take my word for it. Instead read the publicly acknowledged testimony of some of the hundreds of astronauts, military personnel, government insiders, and aerospace executives from such prestigious organizations like Lockheed Skunkworks. You are the public and the public needs to know what is in this book. Enjoy the read.

~ Joseph Shields

Acknowledged: News

Few subjects are more controversial than the topic of UFOs, unidentified flying objects and the possible existence of extraterrestrial life from outside of our planet. The mystery, if proven to be real, would change the course of human history and mankind's fundamental understanding if itself, forever. Therefore, it is a strange reality that this powerful question has already been answered. We are not alone. However, with mountains of evidence and eminently qualified witnesses in both the public and private sector, including the military, that have testified to the existence of this reality; the governments of the world persist in their refusal to acknowledge a formal disclosure of the alien presence here on Earth.

The knowledge that we humans are not the only sentient beings on Earth has been known by animal researchers for decades. Still, to consider human like intelligence outside of humanity remains a taboo concept. Strangely, mankind has a powerful connection to this unacknowledged reality. Most religions and belief systems recognize and are based on the existence of some unearthly influence capable of imparting wisdom, providing comfort, or intervening on our behalf. New translations of the book of Genesis by Hebrew scholars shed light on some of the oldest interactions between possible extraterrestrial lifeforms and humanity. There are many ancient manuscripts that appear to describe such things.

The Sumerian bible, and other ancient writings indicate that aliens were "cast down" here and created man "in their image" and depicts the double helix (double spiral snake). The Sumerians seemed to know of DNA 6,000 years ago. The double snake became the symbol of medicine even now, 6,000 years later! It is called the Caduceus.

Some believe there is evidence of ancient nuclear wars. Such events include Sodom and Gomorrah's destruction, and the "deluge." Physicists have found the fused sand at the Sodom and Gomorrah location indicative of a nuclear blast. And then there is the Mahabharata. This is an ancient Indian "bible" depicting events that differing experts say occurred from 8,000 to 24,000 years ago. Read the "sacred text" for yourself; does it not fit a nuclear war? What else fits a "flying craft unleashing a projectile with all the power of the Universe" and leaving charred human remains? The Mahabharata supposedly says that one area destroyed is where Kashmir is today.

Because stories of strange objects in the skies have been handed down for millennia and have a long history of being depicted in paintings both on canvas and in the form of petroglyphs, what follows should be no surprise. Puzzling objects have been falling out of the sky for quite some time. In 1561, there was a mass sighting of UFO phenomenon above Nuremberg, Germany. It was reported in newspapers and artist Hans Glaser drew a woodcut of it at the time. It describes two immense black cylinders launching many blue and black spheres, blood red crosses, and flying discs. They seem to fight a battle in the sky, it also seems that some of these spheres and objects crashed outside the city. The following is the original account by Hanns Glaser.

"In the morning of April 14, 1561, at daybreak, between 4 and 5 a.m., a dreadful apparition occurred on the sun, and then this was seen in Nuremberg in the city, before the gates and in the country by many men and women.

At first there appeared in the middle of the sun two blood-red semi-circular arcs, just like the moon in its last quarter. And in the sun, above and below and on both sides, the color was blood, there stood a round ball of partly dull, partly black ferrous color. Likewise, there stood on both sides and as a torus about the sun, such blood-red ones and other balls in large number, about three in a line and four in a square, also some alone. In between these globes there were visible a few blood-red crosses, between which there were blood-red strips, becoming thicker to the rear and in the front malleable like the rods of reed-grass, which were intermingled, among them two big rods, one on the right, the other to the left, and within the small and big rods there were three, also four and more globes.

These all started to fight among themselves, so that the globes, which were first in the sun, flew out to the ones standing on both sides, thereafter, the globes standing outside the sun, in the small and large rods, flew into the sun. Besides this the globes flew back and forth among themselves and fought vehemently with each other for over an hour. And when the conflict in and again out of the sun was most intense, they became fatigued to such an extent that they all, as said above, fell from the sun down upon the earth 'as if they all burned' and they then wasted away on the earth with immense smoke. After all this there was something like a black spear, very long and thick, sighted; the shaft pointed to the east, the point pointed west.

Whatever such signs mean, God alone knows. Although we have seen, shortly one after another, many kinds of signs on the heaven, which are sent to us by the almighty God, to bring us to repentance, we still are, unfortunately, so ungrateful that we despise such high signs and miracles of God. Or we speak of them with ridicule and discard them to the wind, in order that God may send us a frightening punishment on account of our ungratefulness. After all, the God-fearing will by no means discard these signs, but will take it to heart as a warning of their merciful Father in heaven, will mend their lives and faithfully beg God, that He may avert His wrath, including the well-deserved punishment on us, so that we may temporarily here and perpetually there, live as his children. For it, may God grant us his help, Amen."

~ **Hanns Glaser**, letter-painter of Nurnberg

According to locals living in Aurora, Texas in 1879, a UFO reportedly crashed on a local farm. An alien body is said to have been buried in an unmarked grave at the local cemetery. There was even a mention of the incident in a local newspaper. So, just take a minute to absorb the fact that UFO's, crashed vehicles, and alien corpses are not exactly a new thing.

The crash that occurred in Roswell, New Mexico On July 8, 1947, was widely reported in newspapers. The Roswell Army Air Field (RAAF) public information officer Walter Haut, issued a press release stating that personnel from the field's **509th Operations Group** had recovered a "flying disc", which had crashed on a ranch near the base. This alone should give the average person reason to believe in the subject.

Recent testimony by government insiders disclosing information about UFO's to the public suggests that aside from UFO crashes like the one at Roswell, there is reason to believe that the intelligences behind these phenomena have deliberately "seeded" various nations with their technology. We know now that it is highly likely that there have been, not one or two, but scores of crashed alien vehicles internationally since the nineteen forties. This information is readily available for researches with a simple Google search on the subject.

"There were all kinds of stuff - small beams about three eights or a half inch square with some sort of hieroglyphics on them that nobody could decipher. These looked something like balsa wood, and were of about the same weight, except that they were of about the same weight, except that they were not wood at all. They were very hard, although flexible, and would not burn. There was a great deal of unusual parchment-like substance which was brown in color and extremely strong, and a great number of small pieces of a metal like tinfoil, except that it wasn't tinfoil."

~ **Lieutenant Colonial Jesse Marcel**, United States Air Force

"I noticed that they were standing around looking at some dead bodies that had fallen to the ground. I think there were others in the machine, which was a kind of metallic...disc. It was not all that big. It seemed to be made of metal that looked like dirty stainless steel. The machine had been split open by explosion or impact."

"I tried to get close to see what the bodies were like. They were all dead as far as I could see and there were bodies inside and outside the vehicle. The ones outside had been tossed out by the impact. They were like humans but they were not humans. The heads were round, the eyes were small, and they had no hair. The eyes were oddly spaced. They were quite small by our standards and their heads were larger in proportion to their bodies than ours. Their clothing seemed to be one-piece and grey in color. You couldn't see any zippers, belts or buttons. They seemed to be all males and there were a number of them. I as close enough to touch them but I didn't - I was escorted away before I could [do so]."

~ **Grady L. Barnett**, civil engineer with the US Soil Conservation Service

Even General Macarthur chimed in on the subject.

"The next war will be an interplanetary war. The nations must someday make a common front against attack by people from other planets."

General Douglas MacArthur

During the time between July 12 to July 29, 1952, over Washington, D.C. there were a series of unidentified flying object reports, over Washington, D.C. This UFO incident, also known as the Washington flap, the Washington National Airport Sightings, or the Invasion of Washington was heavily photographed in color. The images are powerful and show as many as a dozen bright and easily discernable UFO's in a well-organized formation, literally parked in the night skies over The White House. UFO historian Curtis Peebles called the incident "the climax of the 1952 (UFO) flap" - "Never before or after did Project Blue Book and the Air Force undergo such a tidal wave of (UFO) reports."

At 11:40 p.m. on Saturday, July 19, 1952, Edward Nugent, an air traffic controller at Washington National Airport (today Ronald Reagan Washington National Airport), spotted seven objects on his radar. The objects were located 15 miles (24 km) south-southwest of the city; no known aircraft were in the area and the objects were not following any established flight paths. Nugent's

superior, Harry Barnes, a senior air-traffic controller at the airport, watched the objects on Nugent's radarscope. He later wrote," We knew immediately that a very strange situation existed . . . their movements were completely radical compared to those of ordinary aircraft."

At this point, other objects appeared in all sectors of the radarscope; when they moved over the White House and the United States Capitol, Barnes called Andrews Air Force Base, located 10 miles from National Airport. Airman William Brady, who was in the tower, then saw an "object which appeared to be like an orange ball of fire, trailing a tail . . . [it was] unlike anything I had ever seen before."

Lieutenant Colonel Philip James Corso was an American Army officer who published a book called The Day After Roswell, about how his involvement in the research of extraterrestrial technology recovered from the 1947 Roswell UFO Incident. According to him and others, President Dwight Eisenhower had ordered the military to farm out the top-secret development of technology from the recovered alien ship to private American aerospace corporations.

For many years, there have been rumors of Eisenhower meeting extraterrestrials on secret trips to Air Force bases. Some even believe that Eisenhower entered into secret agreements between the United States government and cosmic civilizations. The evidence to support these claims has been sparse. However, Bill Kirklin says he was at Holloman Air Force base when such an event took place, and that although he didn't see anything, his colleagues had.

He remembers the circumstances being strange, because normally the President would get a parade, but the parade for this visit was cancelled the day before he arrived.

Among the peculiar events of the day of Eisenhower's visit, Kirklin recalls that he was part of a strange conversation between two officers, during his coffee break. He remembers it going like this:

Officer 1: "I'm the Officer of the day. Air Force One (the President's plane) came in."

Kirklin: "What happened?"

Officer 1: "He landed, then turned around and stopped." After a pause, the officer added: "We were told to turn off the radar."

Kirklin: "Now why were we asked to turn off the radar?"

Officer 1: "I don't know, we just turned it off."

Officer 2: "I heard that the one that was shot down by Roswell was brought down through radar." (It is assumed by Roswell that the officer meant the alleged crash of a UFO in Roswell, NM.)

After that, he heard the officers continue talking. They talked about seeing an alien autopsy before continuing their discussion on the President's visit.

They discussed two crafts, one landed in front of the President's plane and the other hovered overhead, as if it was protecting the other. The President got out of his plane and walked into the craft on the ground. The President was in the craft for around forty-five minutes before coming out and walking back to his airplane.

The probability that this meeting occurred is greatly increased by the fact that in 2010, retired New Hampshire state representative, Henry McElroy Jr., stated that he was privy to a secret briefing document intended for Eisenhower. This document contained information that aliens were in America and that Eisenhower could meet with them.

"To the best of my memory, this brief was pervaded with a sense of hope, and it informed President Eisenhower of the continued presence of extraterrestrial beings here in the United States of America. The tone of the brief indicated to me that there was no need for concern, since these visitors were in no way causing any harm or had any intentions whatsoever of causing any disruption then or in the future."

What we know historically is that the power of the corporations doing business with our government and the military had grown so great that on Jan. 17, 1961, President Dwight Eisenhower gave the nation a dire warning about what he described as a threat to democracy. He called it the military-industrial complex, a formidable union of defense contractors and the armed forces.

"In the councils of government, we must guard against the acquisition of unwarranted influence, whether sought or unsought, by the military-industrial complex. The potential for the disastrous rise of misplaced power exists, and will persist."

2

Acknowledged: 1960's

On January 31, 1961, John F. Kennedy became the 35th President of the United States. When this happened he instantly became the keeper of the nation's growing extraterrestrial secrets. A little over a year later on July 9, 1962, the government, in a joint effort of the Atomic Energy Commission (AEC) and the Defense Atomic Support Agency, conducted Operation Starfish Prime, a high-altitude nuclear test using a Thor rocket carrying a W49 thermonuclear warhead launched from Johnston Island in the Pacific Ocean. There were many similar attempts that mysteriously failed and some have suggested foul play by forces unknown.

"The US Airforce assures me that UFO's pose no threat to National Security."
~ **President John F Kennedy**

The summer of 1962 was problematic for nuclear weapons aboard Thor rockets. The Bluegill nuclear test on June 4, 1962, was aborted 10 minutes after launch when the missile tracking system failed prior to nuclear detonation; the nuclear device was lost and the Thor destroyed. The original Starfish test on June 20, 1962, failed one minute after launch, again losing the nuclear device and destroying the Thor; radioactive metal and debris rained over Johnston Island. The summer concluded with extensive plutonium contamination of Johnston Island and following the failed Bluegill Prime nuclear test on July 26, 1962, which was aborted on the launch pad after the Thor engine malfunctioned on ignition.

Why would our government be so intent on such tests when interfering with Earth's magnetic field is capable of producing most dire of consequences? The magnetic field protects Earth from all sorts of energetic particles from the Sun and from more distant sources which sometimes emit massive fluxes of high-energy particles. Some scientists have found that even the rocket exhausts have caused significant damage to the protective ozone layer around the Earth. You could argue that there was no scientific basis for exploding fission bombs in outer space since it risked endangering life on the planet.

The stress of coping with all of these missile failures must have taken its toll on President Kennedy and if history has taught us anything it's true that he had an ongoing extramarital affair with actress Marilyn Monroe. In fact, it seems that he shared Monroe with his brother, U.S. Attorney General Robert Kennedy. Thus, Monroe's untimely death from a phenobarbital overdose administered rectally and under mysterious circumstances must have made this a very difficult time. However, a recently discovered CIA document of wiretaps of Marilyn Monroe and her friends shortly before her suspicious death on August 5 1962 reveal a long suspected conspiracy theory is likely legitimate.

The wiretap document reveal that Monroe was planning to give a press conference about what President Kennedy had told her of a visit to an undisclosed Air Force facility where he saw the debris of a crashed UFO. The Monroe wiretap document was first leaked in 1992 to a UFO researcher, and was made public in 1994. Right up until her suspicious and much-discussed death in 1962 Marilyn Monroe was under surveillance. The FBI were keeping tabs on her, the Mafia had a private detective bug her phone and house, and this memo seems to confirm that the CIA were also monitoring her. This is what the alleged CIA wiretap document, dated August 3, 1962, had to say about Monroe's knowledge of Kennedy and UFOs.

Dated August 3rd, 1962, two days before she died, it references wiretaps of conversations between 'reporter Dorothy Kilgallen and her close friend, Howard Rothberg' and 'Marilyn Monroe and Attorney General Robert Kennedy'. It is not clear whether these wiretaps were the CIA's own work, or whether this came from the FBI or from the taps run by Fred Otash on behalf of Jimmy Hoffa. The memo lists five pieces of apparently relevant information gleaned from the surveillance.

1. Rothberg discussed the apparent comeback of subject with Kilgallen and the break up with the Kennedys. Rothberg told Kilgallen that she was attending Hollywood parties hosted by the "inner circle" among Hollywood's elite and was becoming the talk of the town again. Rothberg indicated in so many words, that she had secrets to tell, no doubt arising from her trysts with the President and the Attorney General. One such "secret" mentions the visit by the President at a secret air base for the purpose of inspecting things from outer space. Kilgallen replied that she knew what might be the source of visit. In the mid-fifties Kilgallen learned of secret effort by US and UK governments to identify the origins of crashed spacecraft and dead bodies, from a British government official. Kilgallen believed the story may have come from the New Mexico story in the late forties. Kilgallen said that if the story is true, it would cause terrible embarrassment for Jack and his plans to have NASA put men on the moon.

2. Subject repeatedly called the Attorney General and complained about the way she was being ignored by the President and his brother.

3. Subject threatened to hold a press conference and would tell all.

4. Subject referred to "bases" in Cuba and knew of the President's plan to kill Castro.

5. Subject referred to her "diary of secrets" and what the newspapers would do with such disclosures.

The implications of the Monroe wiretap document being genuine are astounding. It reveals that only one day before her death, Monroe was planning a press conference that would reveal what President Kennedy had confidentially told her about UFOs. The fact that the CIA was monitoring her and wiretapping her phone calls, directly implicates the CIA in her suspicious death and the cover-up of information concerning UFOs.

The sixties brought war in Vietnam and the NASA space program that would with Apollo 11, on 20 July 1969, see us land on the moon. With this venture into space came reports from American astronauts that they too had seen UFO's. Encouraging the speculation about the nature of their sightings came a trickle of statements and conjecture about the possible nature of their experiences with objects under intelligent control not of this Earth.

Here is what some of our astronauts had to say:

"Mission Control, please be informed, there is a Santa Claus."

~ **Astronaut Captain James Lovell**, Apollo 8 Commander, 1968. He made this transmission after coming around the far side of the Moon on the Apollo 8 mission. "Santa Claus" was a codeword used to indicate a UFO.

"I believe that these extraterrestrial vehicles and their crews are visiting this planet from other planets which obviously are a little more technically advanced than we are here on earth."

~ **Astronaut Air Force Colonel L. Gordon Cooper**, Mercury 7

"We all know that UFOs are real. All we need to ask is where do they come from."

~ **Astronaut Captain Edgar D. Mitchell**, Apollo 14

"I've been asked [about UFOs] and I've said publicly I thought they were somebody else, some other civilization."

~ **Astronaut Captain Eugene Cernan**, Apollo 17

And from NASA:

"I've been convinced for a long time that the flying saucers are real and interplanetary. In other words, we are being watched by beings from outer space."

~ **Albert M. Chop**, NASA deputy public relations director.

3

Acknowledged: 1970's

The nineteen seventies brought continued change and public knowledge of top-secret government programs that explored the boundaries of human consciousness. MK Ultra and Stargate were two of these endeavors.

Project MK Ultra, the CIA's mind control program, was the code name given to a program of experiments on human subjects, at times illegal, designed to identify and develop drugs and procedures to be used in interrogations and torture, and control human behavior which, although it began in the 1950s, officially halted in 1973. Something President Bill Clinton's apologized publicly for on Oct. 3, 1995.

"Thousands of government-sponsored experiments did take place at hospitals, universities, and military bases around our nation. Some were unethical, not only by today's standards, but by the standards of the time in which they were conducted. They failed both the test of our national values and the test of humanity. The United States of America offers a sincere apology to those of our citizens who were subjected to these experiments, to their families, and to their communities. When the government does wrong, we have a moral responsibility to admit it."

~ **President William Jefferson Clinton**

Considering the controversial nature of experimenting on unsuspecting American citizens and using American soldiers to explore psychic abilities, we are left to wonder why? Why spend so much money on such ruthless and esoteric research into human consciousness?

The nineteen eighties and nineties brought us the space shuttle program and with it astronaut witnesses and video from both the shuttle and the international space station or ISS.

"Mission control, we have a UFO pacing our position, request instructions."

~ **Astronaut Colonel Cady Coleman**, Ph.D., NASA Space Shuttle Astronaut, Shuttle Mission STS-73

"For many years, I have lived with a secret, in a secrecy imposed on all specialists in astronautics. I can now reveal that every day, in the USA, our radar instruments capture objects of form and composition unknown to us. And there are thousands of witness reports and a quantity of documents to prove this, but nobody wants to make them public. Why? Because authority is afraid that people may think of God knows what kind of horrible invaders. So, the password still is: We have to avoid panic by all means"

"I was furthermore a witness to an extraordinary phenomenon, here on this planet Earth. It happened a few months ago in Florida. There I saw with my own eyes a defined area of ground being consumed by flames, with four indentations left by a flying object which had descended in the middle of a field. Beings had left the craft (there were other traces to prove this). They seemed to have studied topography, they had collected soil samples and, eventually, they returned to where they had come from, disappearing at enormous speed...I happen to know that authority did just about everything to keep this incident from the press and TV, in fear of a panicky reaction from the public"

~ **Astronaut Major L. Gordon Cooper**

"At no time, when the astronauts were in space were they alone: there was a constant surveillance by UFOs."

~ **Astronaut Scott Carpenter**, NASA

I believe, and I scientifically am certain, that there are endless other living forms out there, including intelligent sentient beings. I do know that there are entire universes of living forms out there.

~ **Astronaut Story Musgrave**, M.D., Ph.D., awarded 20 honorary doctorates, NASA Challenger

"The phenomenon of UFOs is real. I know that there are scientific organizations which study the problem."
~ **Former Soviet President Mikhail Gorbachev** on 26th April 1990.

"This is the first sighting in Zimbabwe where airborne pilots have tried to intercept a UFO. As far as my Air Staff is concerned, we believe implicitly that the unexplained UFOs are from civilizations beyond our planet."
~ **Air Commodore David Thorne,** Director of General Operations for the Zimbabwe Air Force in 1985.

"The Air Force has arrived at the conclusion that a certain number of anomalous phenomena has been produced in Belgian airspace. The numerous testimonies of ground observations, reinforced by the reports of the night March 30-31 (1990) have led us to face the hypothesis that a certain number of unauthorized aerial activities have taken place.

The day will undoubtedly come when the phenomenon will be observed with the technological means of detection and collection that won't leave a single doubt about its origin. This should lift a part of the veil that has covered the mystery for a long time; a mystery that continues to be present. But it exists, it is real, and that is an important conclusion."

~ **Colonel Wilfred De Brouwer**, Chief of Operations for the Belgian Air Force

"It is impossible for any man-made machine to make a sudden appearance in front of a jumbo jet that is flying 910 kilometers per hour and to remain in steady formation paralleling our aircraft. ... Honestly, we were simply breathtaking."

~ **Kenju Terauchi, Japan** Airlines pilot in 1986.

"I've been convinced for a long time that the flying saucers are real and interplanetary. In other words, we are being watched by beings from outer space."

~ **Albert M. Chop**, deputy public relations director NASA

n 1979 Maurice Chatelain, former chief of NASA Communications Systems confirmed that Astronaut Neil Armstrong reported seeing two UFOs on the rim of a crater. He had this to say, "The encounter was common knowledge in NASA, but nobody has talked about it until now." "...all Apollo and Gemini flights were followed, both at a distance and sometimes also quite closely, by space vehicles of extraterrestrial origin - flying saucers, or UFOs, if you want to call them by that name. Every time it occurred, the astronauts informed Mission Control, who then ordered absolute silence."

UFOs are seen daily on NASA's live video feeds. During a 2005 spacewalk outside the International Space Station, astronaut Leroy Chiao reported seeing lights in a formation he described as "in a line" and "almost like an upside-down check mark".

In August 2013, according to NASA TV, astronaut Captain Christopher Cassidy of the United States Navy saw a UFO float past the International Space Station near its Progress 52 cargo ship. United States Navy Captain

Scott Joseph Kelly not only reported several UFO's while on the ISS, but he also took a picture of them and released it to the public. Now remember, Captain Kelly holds the record for the most days spent in space by any human. You can imagine that he knows what he is seeing.

Clark McClelland, former NASA engineer worked as an aerospace engineer for 35 years from 1958 to 1992. He claims to have observed an eight to nine-feet while he was monitoring it from the Kennedy Space Centre in Cape Canaveral, Florida. While monitoring an unspecified top secret mission from the space center's launch control center on a 27-inch video screen, he saw the "alien" standing upright on two legs in the space shuttle payload bay, interacting with the two tethered US astronauts and watched it for one minute and seven seconds. He also claims to have seen on another occasion a UFO at the rear of the shuttle. He said, "I know an ET and alien craft when I see them. Aliens are here on Earth, they walk among us. They may have been implanted into our various Earth governments."

"In my official status, I cannot comment on ET contact. However, personally, I can assure you, we are not alone!"

~ **Astronaut Charles J. Camarda**, Ph.D., NASA, Space Shuttle mission STS-114

"For nearly 50 years, the secrecy apparatus within the United States Government has kept from the public UFO and alien contact information." "We have contact with alien cultures."

~ **Astronaut Brian T. O'Leary**, NASA, Scientist

So here we are, it's now 2017 and almost seventy years since the bulk of what we know our government has been involved with regarding UFO's began. The United States is only about one hundred and forty-one years into is existence as a sovereign nation. We have witnessed the industrial revolution and are now entering a new millennium and our nation's best and brightest Astronauts have all acknowledged that UFO's and extraterrestrial life exists. The cat has been out of the bag for a long time and the government knows this. In fact, as you will learn, they are doing what they can to tell the public without directly coming out and saying that, "we are not alone."

4

Acknowledged: White House

In November of 2016 the world learned that White House Chief of Staff and senior presidential advisor John D. Podesta was communicating with a team of U.S. Military and private sector advisors, led by Major General William N. McCasland, to publicly acknowledge the United States governments involvement with UFO's. General McCasland was, until 2013, the Commander of the Air Force Research Laboratory located at Wright-Patterson Air Force Base, in Dayton, Ohio.

During 2015, musician Tom DeLonge announced to the world that he was working with a team of government, corporate, and researchers who were supporting him to disclose, through a series of books and media projects called, "Sekret Machines", designed to educate young people about the nation's history related to UFO's and massive unacknowledged special access programs (USAPs) costing trillions of dollars that the American public have unknowingly funded over the past seventy years. General McCasland, at the helm, put together a ten-person panel of "Deep Throat Advisors" from the military, aerospace, research facilities and medicine to educate and feed information to DeLonge for his books and documentaries.

White House Chief of Staff and Senior Advisor to President Barack Obama John Podesta expressed disappointment in February 2015 that his time in the White House didn't result in the revelation of the existence of UFOs stating, "Finally, my biggest failure of 2014: Once again not securing the disclosure of the UFO files." However, in April, Podesta said that Hillary Clinton had promised him that she would declassify all documents pertaining to extraterrestrials if elected president.

In March 2016, the personal email account of Podesta, the chairman of Hillary Clinton's 2016 U.S. presidential campaign, was compromised in a data breach, and a collection of his emails, many of which were work-related, were stolen. Cybersecurity researchers as well as the United States government attributed responsibility for the breach, which was accomplished via a spear-phishing attack, to the hacking group Fancy Bear, affiliated with Russian intelligence services.

Some or all the Podesta emails were subsequently obtained by WikiLeaks, which published over 20,000 pages of emails, from Podesta, in October and November 2016. Included in these released email communications were a series of correspondences between a select group of government, military insiders, and UFO researchers. Also, included in leaked emails was the full PDF file of the book Sekret Machines Book 1: Chasing Shadows by "UFO Researcher of the Year" Tom DeLonge and NY Times bestselling academic AJ Hartley.

Cybersecurity experts interviewed by PolitiFact believe the emails are unaltered. An investigation by U.S. intelligence agencies reported that the files obtained by WikiLeaks during the U.S. election contained no "evident forgeries." What was revealed is evidence of a secret group of insiders within our government planning the release of the most vital information in the history of mankind; UFO's are not only real but our government believes they are malevolent.

The WikiLeaks emails brought much of Mr. Tom Delonge's work to the fore, and showed conclusively that he was actively consulting with the Whitehouse Chief of Staff, John Podesta and Maj. Gen. William N. McCasland, among others. Mr. Delonge said in the messages that he had been communicating with high-ranking officials in the US government regarding a secret program designed to disclose information related to the complex UFO phenomenon. Many of these contacts were revealed in the details of these email chains.

In the Podesta emails, leaked by WikiLeaks, DeLonge reached out to Hillary Clinton's campaign chairman, in October 2015, to set up a Washington, D.C. meeting between them and two people "in charge of most fragile divisions, as it relates to Classified Science and DOD topics." He described these people as "A-Level officials."

One of the officials, a January 2016 email revealed, was General William McCasland, Commander of the Air Force Research Laboratory at Wright-Patterson Air Force Base in Ohio, where pieces from the Roswell UFO crash were purportedly shipped. DeLonge wrote to Podesta in a second email saying, "[McCasland] not only knows what I'm trying to achieve, he helped assemble my advisory team...He's a very important man."

While another leaked email, a calendar notification, suggested that Podesta did schedule a time to meet with DeLonge and Maj. General McCasland.

The release of the emails instantly cast light on the innerworkings of the group preparing to make formal UFO disclosure public and caused DeLonge to censor his media communications and radio interviews.

DeLonge wrote on Instagram, nearly two weeks after his emails to Podesta leaked, "WikiLeaks really messed some important stuff up." However, he had already conducted over twelve hours of radio interviews and, as you'll find in this briefing document, the truth has already been revealed.

5

Acknowledged: The General

Major General William N. McCasland is the Commander, Air Force Research Laboratory, Wright-Patterson Air Force Base, Ohio. He is responsible for managing the Air Force's $2.2 billion science and technology program as well as additional customer funded research and development of technology.

He is also responsible for a global workforce of approximately 10,800 people in the laboratory's component technology directorates, 711th Human Performance Wing and the Air Force Office of Scientific Research. In fact, he stated to Tom DeLonge that he oversaw all the UFO stuff. When the Roswell crash happened, they shipped the alien vehicle wreckage and bodies to the laboratory at Wright Patterson Air Force Base. Maj. General McCasland told DeLonge that oversaw that exact laboratory up to a couple years ago.

General McCasland was commissioned in 1979 after graduating from the U.S. Air Force Academy with a Bachelor of Science degree in astronautical engineering. He has served in a wide variety of space research, acquisition and operations roles within the Air Force and the National Reconnaissance Office. He commanded the Phillips site of Air Force Research Laboratory at Kirtland AFB, N.M., and served as Vice Commander of the Ogden Air Logistics Center and the Space and Missile Systems Center. He previously served at the Pentagon, first as the Director, Space Acquisition, in the Office of the Secretary of the Air Force, and then as Director of Special Programs, Office of the Under Secretary of Defense for Acquisition, Technology and Logistics. General McCasland holds a doctorate degree in astronautical engineering from the Massachusetts Institute of Technology where he studied under a John and Fannie Hertz Foundation fellowship.

Is the top-secret contact referred to in Tom Delonge's novel SeKret Machines and in the plethora of interviews he has given Maj. Gen. William N. McCasland, the Commander of the Air Force Research Laboratory, Wright-Patterson Air Force Base, Ohio? Let's assume he is. One thing is certain. He was never intended to be quoted directly (DeLonge only refers to "The General") in statements he has made and John Podesta isn't talking.

6

Acknowledged: NASA

It was during a two-hour meeting at the NASA Ames Research Center, one of ten NASA field centers, located in the heart of California's Silicon Valley, that a NASA representative first introduced DeLonge to a man who he refers to as "The General".

The first time DeLonge met "The General", the General said to him, "It was the cold war and every single day we lived under the threat of nuclear war, every single day we believed and really thought in the deepest part of our souls that nuclear war could happen at any given moment. And somewhere in those years we found a life form and everything that we did and every decision we made with that life form was because of the consciousness at that time."

The General later stated, "I've made calls about you. You better be careful. If someone comes by and asks you to get into a car don't fucking get in, this is very serious stuff you are getting involved in."

The General then sent a message by email saying, "I want you to be (at this location) next to the Pentagon at this day and time and you are going to be meeting someone from the CIA". Following that there was another a meeting set up in San Diego.

Delonge spoke to the "The General" many times and this man's overriding concern was always what's best for the free Republic. There was a time when the UFO's were turning our weapons on so that Russia would fire theirs first and then he said, "there are heroes in Russia that decided not to fire those weapons."

Following this first meeting, "The General" went out and got the advisors for him, specifically, ten advisors in space, intelligence, biowarfare, engineering, medicine, technology. Later he Flew to Air Force Space Command and they brought in Space intelligence people for him to talk to. When he asked them about crashes in the forties they responded, "why just the forties"?

He has stated that he's been in "email chains with hundreds of scientists from the Jet Propulsion Laboratory and different universities around the country," resulting in his phone being tapped and his security being threatened. He learned many things, all of which he has publicly discussed are revealed in this document, including the fact that the government has leaked and created ridicule over the years to kill interest in the subject and now they finally want people to know. If people knew what the stakes are the whole world would change. Yes, we have cracked gravity and are building craft that control gravity. He was told that.

7

Acknowledged: "The Others"

"The Others" is the term all the government, military and all the scientific advisors use to describe the aliens and they are gods. Their strategy is to get humans to fight among ourselves.

The top, top echelon of the U.S. government and governments around the world know that our cultures obsession with violence and negative things is very wrong and is feeding this negative interdimensional presence which wants us to feel this negativity.

They instigate war among mankind, the government knows this and is very aware that this intelligence is turning countries against each other based on religion. His sources have stated that we don't want them knowing our vulnerabilities or the advancements we have made. We are trying to keep it secret so that we don't create a conflict where other people are concerned with the manipulation of the Others.

DeLonge: "Cattle mutilations and human abductions are involved and are part of the UFO phenomenon and I've been told this by my advisors. It's an act of war being perpetrated by the Others, these alien entities.

Recently one third of our NATO weapons were shut off in our oceans worldwide several months ago by The Others. This alien force. This happened around December of 2015."

DeLonge, working together with John Podesta and Maj. Gen. William N. McCasland, a panel of "Deep Throat Advisors" was created. DeLonge has publicly stated, "I have 10 people that are working with me at the highest levels of the aerospace industry, Department of Defense, NASA and the military. Everything about the Podesta WikiLeaks emails confirms this fact and direct involvement by the highest possible levels of the United States Government. Disclosure has happened and everything we now know is being presented here.

During DeLonge's first disclosure meetings, several secret advisors including "The General", said things to DeLonge like, "When I was a kid I used to read a lot of Greek mythology." or "Look at Greek mythology." Apparently, the Greek Gods were real and were aliens. However, he went on to say, "I think that's about one race and there are multiple races. It was during ancient Greek times when they made themselves very visible, the Greek alphabet, democracy, architecture etc., that's where it all came from."

Deep state factions of the United States government have discovered and established as fact that there exists a quantum intelligence that pervades our very existence. These are transdimensional intelligences from other dimensions while some are none corporeal, there are others that have physical bodies. This intelligent presence is at the core of the UFO phenomenon. The presence manifests a plethora of physical and nonphysical entities that the government refers to as "The Others". There are high level groups within the DOD and national security divisions of our country keeping all this secret because of global security. This has been the case for seventy years.

The General: "they are real, they exist." How do they work? "consciousness."

Delonge: "The government has known about UFO's for decades and has replicated some of the technology"

"I was told there were crashes and we created a crash program, much bigger than the Manhattan Project or the Apollo Program, to figure out how this stuff worked and how to build our own defense system against it should there be more," Since the 1950's the government of The

United States, in concert with nations like Russia, Germany and France, have been secretly developing advanced technologies to combat this alien threat. Delonge explained, "we've been building something secret to help protect us.'"

"These things have weighed heavily on me, I've been told more than four different times to be careful not to do or say certain things."

"Our government has made a commitment to do whatever it takes to protect the planet from these forces. I learned that Henry Kissinger, after he became involved in the UFO matter, became a recluse."

"There have been, throughout time, events designed to change the course of history, crashes designed to give technology to opposing sides during wars etc."

"genetics play a major role in what is going on."

"I was told that this phenomenon can manipulate the minds of men including those charged with investigating it."

"There are lots of different races of extraterrestrial beings and they don't all look like us. Some of them don't like us and we don't like them."

Scientist Advisor: "Some of the lifeforms are clones and some are mechanical. Some are AI and don't have souls. Some are biological...Some of these entities we've recovered were found to have technology in the back of their brains presumably transmitting everything they saw, heard and did back to some unknown source"

"You can't think of space and time as separate entities, so you see, the curvature in Space-Time can be exploited by applying pressure"

CIA Advisor: "The story is one of cosmology, religion, scientific break throughs, and defense systems you couldn't even dream of. It's all been paid for by the petrodollar which is why we have kept the technology that could free us from using oil a secret; because we needed this flow of money to fund the deep black international "alien defense project." We don't want these entities behind the UFO phenomenon to be aware of the technology we truly have here on earth. It's been purely strategic. The technology isn't being hidden from us but rather, it's being from them. Scary stuff. There are things about this phenomenon involving the oceans, viruses and a lot of scary stuff."

DeLonge: "To hide what the governments are building in secret, they blame it on spaceships and aliens, but it's all to hide what we're really building, something that is real but is exotic and esoteric, and it's all part of a plan. And as we find out that the phenomenon is real, they're hoping it won't be as bad as we thought it was, because we were scared along the way "

Even more amazing is the fact that this quantum presence manifests itself in the form of both physical and noncorporal entities which encompasses all paranormal phenomenon, from ghosts and apparitions, to demonic entities and poltergeist phenomenon.

Government sources have also deliberately revealed that these entities possess the ability to influence the minds of human beings. Alarmingly, these same sources have stated that this phenomenon is in fact malevolent.

All the ancient religions were written down based on witnessing this phenomenon in various forms. Governments of the world watched the phenomenon and tried to replicate the technology, but they did it in secret. Their agenda was first to "comprehend and outwit this intelligence before we (they) educate (ed) the public about this phenomenon "they were discovering and then to develop a defense against it. There are high level groups within the DOD and national security divisions of our country keeping all this secret because of global security. So, the governments are fighting each other with these pieces of technology. But within those little skirmishes, the phenomenon is still here, and it's much more advanced than us.

DeLonge's confidential advisors have stated that our human behaviors were designed so we would hate each other so that we would be distracted from the extraterrestrial presence and we have been led astray.

This is being fueled by matter displacement, holograms and illusion. The top echelon in the government knows that we are being conditioned to violence on purpose and until we stop this, the world will not change. Violence and negativity changes the human frequency of how you feel and this lifeform that has been identified by the United States Government wants you to feel this way. This life form feeds off negative psychic energy.

They have always been on Earth whether in a small group or an outpost, one group goes back to before Atlantis. There are other groups outside the solar system that are just bad news.

We have back channel communications working on this alien threat with countries that on the political surface appear to be adversaries. Behind the scenes, we are working together on weaponry designed to handle this alien threat. This is what has prevented world war three from occurring over the past seventy years.

They are coming and scanning our missile silos and turning our missiles on. The nuclear weaponry we had developed we gave to the Russians during the cold war.

According to Delonge, the government had originally planned to slowly release the information to the public, but never did. Instead, they have disseminated disinformation and have ridiculed the topic, to keep people off the trail of what is really going on.

"There is a lot of private corporate money involved in funding elements of the research and development into these retrieved technologies and this is done in large part to help compartmentalize and protect secrets since information from private corporations cannot be accessed by FOIA requests"

"It's a really complex game that's been played, especially since the '80s, the CIA has been very interested in the UFO civilian research groups, with the intention of being in control over all the research and the public awareness. It was a psychological operation. They were very scared of Americans being gullible and having Russia come in and repeat a War of the Worlds type scenario. So, the CIA said, "We better get in there and make everyone go crazy, but at least it's controlled, and when we're in charge we can slowly let people know the phenomenon is real, but, 'Don't worry -- we've been building something secret to help protect us.'"

8

Acknowledged: Religion and Consciousness

DeLonge: I was told, "Humans were genetically designed to organize around a priestly class and religion has been used by these interdimensional hostile forces to keep humans at each other's throats, occupied with war; it's not all good. People must question the idea of personal sovereignty we are at the mercy of superhuman forces attempting to steer this planet in one direction or another. This group are the angels of the Bible while there is another group that are the Devil of the Bible."

"I've learned there is a strong link between what people think demons are and the UFO phenomenon. We might be an agricultural product. Some of these entities our government is working to protect us from are feeding off fear and the negative psychic energy created by war."

The General: "Would the link of aliens creating man then creating God to keep us in our place be something of interest? Something that doesn't like man and is jealous of man and has a plan."

These interdimensional entities, of which many types have been identified, can influence our minds, implant thoughts, and can be accessed by meditation. "If we all begin meditating to contact alien phenomenon, this might be a major security risk. One man's demon is another man's alien."

"There is this tension between our true nature as humans and these entities that want to keep us from achieving our more God like potential as human beings. Some of them feed off of negative psychic energy."

"The Paper Clip NAZI, William Pelly, said he was in contact with the space beings."

The Scientist: "Extinct ancient civilizations are evidence of those who that did not obey these alien Gods". We are dealing with forces that are hostile to us. "Empire building and resource extraction...is what they (the aliens) are doing."

Delonge has stated he has been told that the UFO phenomenon is tied to human consciousness. The Universe itself has all things in it and contains interesting properties and lifeforms. The UFO phenomenon has a lot to do with humanity as a lifeform. There are specific frequencies that emanate from human beings. The UFO phenomenon is interested in the bad things you feel and brings a lot of bad things. Over the years, the United States Government has found this out and are trying to understand it. At every turn, our scientific researchers and engineers are finding out something new.

There are these heroic amazing people internationally, trying to understand things humanity has never had to understand before. There are very good people changing their pants every day who are losing sleep and are becoming alcoholics because they must deal with these amazing and crazy things. We are constantly trying to accelerate our understanding of these things.

One thing we have learned is that this phenomenon is highly sensitive to positivity and elevated human thought. For example, if you wake up and are being abducted and if you call out the name of Jesus or Buddha, the positive energy will apparently stop an abduction.

There are these spaceships that have crashed, biological bodies and technology that we have back engineered and it's all tied into human consciousness. Just imagine this amazing reality being revealed that there are physicists studying crashed vehicles, medical doctors studying abductees and experiencers, aerospace experts sending up things to take down these alien vehicles, and psychologists studying people having poltergeist experiences etc. These people are talking to each other and are involved in this disclosure process.

The Scientist: "Extinct ancient civilizations are evidence of those who that did not obey these alien Gods". We are dealing with forces that are hostile to us. "Empire building and resource extraction...is what they (the aliens) are doing."

They have always been on Earth whether in a small group or an outpost, one group goes back to before Atlantis. There are other groups outside the solar system that are just bad news.

DeLonge: "I was told that this phenomenon can manipulate the minds of men including those charged with investigating it."

"There are lots of different races of extraterrestrial beings and they don't all look like us. Some of them don't like us and we don't like them."

"The Others" is the term they use to describe the aliens and they are gods! Their strategy is to get humans to fight among ourselves. They instigate war among, the government knows and is very aware that this intelligence is turning countries against each other based on religion.

We don't want them knowing our vulnerabilities or the advancements we have made. We are trying to keep it secret so that we don't create a conflict where other people are concerned with the manipulation of the Others. What has evolved because of this phenomenon is a multi-level chess game between nations. What is the real reason Chinas defense budget has tripled over the past few years? And North Korea?

Cattle mutilations and human abductions are involved and are part of the UFO phenomenon and I've been told this by my advisors. It's an act of war being perpetrated by the Others, these alien entities.

The purpose of the UFO and extraterrestrial phenomenon has been to seed cultures by way of contact with the predesigned purpose of fragmenting mankind. It's all been a big experiment perpetrated on the inhabitants of the planet earth. All paranormal phenomenon is directly connected to this and are interconnected.

DeLonge: "There is a disparity between compartments as to how long they have been visiting us. Some officials believe Atlantis was real and something is very important about that time frame and who the humans were at that time frame."

What Do We Know About the Aliens? Well, they are saying that the UFO's have a hive mind and are like clones and worship their own technology. They cannot combat higher consciousness and our use of technology like I phones, cell phones etc. prevents us from protecting ourselves psychically from them. The United States Government are trying to figure out how society can snap themselves out of this connection to technology.

This interdimensional presence is very interested in human consciousness. There are individuals who have managed to attract UFO's by meditating with some success. Dr. Steven Macon Greer, an American retired medical doctor and ufologist who founded the Center for the Study of Extraterrestrial Intelligence thinks he has developed a way of communicating with these entities he calls the CE-5 protocol. CE-5 is a term describing a fifth category of close encounters with Extraterrestrial Intelligence (ETI), characterized by mutual, bilateral communication rather than unilateral contact. However, like with OUIJI boards and seances this consciousness, according to DeLonge's deep throat advisors, "plays with you and you don't want to meditate an invitation. There isn't one type of UFO as there isn't one type of human being.", said disclosure advisors.

The human spirituality component of positive feelings of love and happiness is important and the government knows it. Bad vibes are real. Elevated human consciousness repels negative things.

DeLonge says, "All the ancient myths are right and true. The powers that be, PhDs and high ranking people know this and that the Universe is magical." The issue is that no one is addressing the fact that there is no mechanism of educating humanity about this phenomenon which is what both Delonge and Dr. Greer are attempting to do. People are worshiping aliens because of television programs and motion pictures and that's what happens when there is an information vacuum and that's why disclosure is important.

Where this research and the control of these programs exists, and are managed is a different type of mechanism. The entire globe is involved and the U.S.A. is the leader in the managing of the UFO extraterrestrial phenomenon because we are the first country with a free mind and a free people.

This is an international project hidden in by the deep state that has been financed in trillions of dollars internationally. This is science and research on a scale that dwarfs the Manhattan Project or the Apollo Project. Imagine seventy years of international collaboration within a hidden scientific community that knows no financial limits whatsoever.

Delonge: "How do you think we finance the defense for this subject....? The petrol dollar.... oil. That's the secret. Big Oil finances the research and the subject is hidden because we do not want the UFO Entities to know we are, as a planet, financing black projects so that we can, as a planet, defend ourselves against malevolent extraterrestrial civilizations that are a danger to mankind.

The technology isn't hidden from us. They don't want the UFO to know what we have accomplished. Our breakthroughs are a competitive advantage in the UFO battlefield and we keep them secret from the UFO's."

It's not going to be the president or congress that discloses this information. The government isn't in charge of the UFO topic in the way you would expect. There are a few key and decision makers that bear this burden for society so society can thrive carefree. Do not hate the government. There are heroes in the government dealing with these things in a way that protects us.

Has there been confirmation of the existence of Cryptoterrestrials, an alien humanoid species indigenous to the Earth, possibly a sister race?

Delonge: How does something that doesn't exist in this dimension....as we know it can create a craft that looks very physical... and probably is.

The Scientist "Using Nano fabrication, atomic layer by atomic layer, with durable Nano texturing and quantum entanglement properties and of course powered by the polarizable vacuum. The same methods that Cryptoterrestrials use."

As for nuclear weapons and the Cold War, these UFO's showed up everywhere once we started playing with nuclear weapons because nuclear weapons mess up alien craft. That's why they showed up in great numbers.

Delonge said, he was told, "During the entire cold war we were working with the Soviet Union on the UFO alien issue. The public never knew and that's why there was never a nuclear war between our nations." During the eighties, Reagan and Gorbachev were working together on this issue.

We are dealing with things we always thought were magic, myth, and understanding this is going to cause humanity to explode to a different level. There is a God but it's not a God that looks like Buddha, it's an infinite beautiful energy that creates black holes, binary star systems stars.

It's the way Einstein described it, beautiful love consciousness that communicates directly connected with all living creatures. That's how the Universe works. Behind all the high security, that is all the head scientists wanted to talk about. For seventy some years the government has been trying to find ways for society to comprehend what is going on in a way that won't destroy it.

The Scientist: "the Universe is teaming with life, organic beings, super human intelligence, weird bands of light that swim in space that are conscious, amoeba's swimming in space that are conscious."

He too has learned through his many government insiders that part of the reason the ETI presence has been kept secret is that one of the first questions would be, "How are they getting here?" It is through zero point or quantum vacuum energy generation systems. And it is those are the energy systems he wants to see us develop and bring out to the public so that we may have a world of pollution free, sustainable abundance.

With scores if not hundreds of military, government, and scientific insiders coming forward the lid is being blown off the secrecy needed to conceal this information.

There are "senior scientists from Lockheed Martin talking about the reality of this stuff, guys that hold 30 patents and guys that work underground out in the Nevada test sites in Area 51,"

"We already have the means to travel among the stars, these technologies are locked up in black projects. Anything you can imagine, we already know how to do it."

"We already have the technology to take ET home. There are two types of UFOs — the ones we build and the ones 'they' build. All points in space and time are connected. That's how it works."
~ **Ben Rich**, Director of Lockheed Skunk Works 1975-1991

"When I was working with the Skunkworks with Kelly Johnson, we signed an agreement with the government to keep very quiet about this... Anti-gravitational research was going on. We know that there were some captured craft from 1947 in Roswell, they were real. And, yes, we really did get some technology from them. And, yes, we really did put it to work. We knew each other from what we call an unseen industry. We can term it black, deep black, or hidden. There was no question that there were beings from outside the planet.

We got these things from the aliens that are handhold scanners that scan the body and determine what the condition is. We can also treat from the same scanner. I can tell you personally that we've been working on them. And we have ones that can diagnose and cure cancer. One of the purposes I had for founding my technology corporation in 1998 was to bring forth these technologies that can clean the air and can help get rid of the toxins, and help reduce the need for so much fossil fuel. Yes, it is time. I can tell you personally that it has already started."

~ **Don Phillips, Lockheed Skunkworks Engineer USAF, and CIA Contractor**

9

Acknowledged: The 12 FACTS

1) *The United States Government has identified an interdimensional intelligence* and parallel worlds containing entities that are responsible for the UFO phenomenon, alien abductions, cattle mutilations, and virtually all paranormal phenomenon imaginable on this planet including ghosts, demonic poltergeist activity, orbs, and even things like spontaneous healing.
2) This interdimensional intelligence is both physical and noncorporal. This intelligence is consciousness based, and can influence the human mind. has taken a malevolent interest in the planet Earth, manipulating humanity and are interested in the psychic energy created by war.
3) This interdimensional intelligence has seeded the planet Earth by way of these crashed vehicles, lifeforms, and technology beginning in the 1920's.

We have been deliberately given this technology by design and the U.S. Government is aware of it.

4) The United States Government has acquired possession of crashed vehicles and more than one of these interdimensional life forms. Some of these physical lifeforms are organic while others appear to have been created and have technology integrated into the brain that appear to allow monitoring by a controlling intelligence.

5) The United States Government has been involved in a seventy-year deep state investigation of this phenomenon in cooperation with the nations of Russia, France, Germany to name a few.

6) North Korea, Iran, China are being manipulated by these alien entities, have very advanced technology because of UFO crashes, and we are aware of this.

7) Many of these governments have, for seventy years, under the leadership of the United States Government, been involved in a scientific effort to create a weapons technology capable of defending the planet Earth against these malevolent forces.

8) This scientific effort has been financed by the international perpetuation of the petrodollar. Although we have long possessed the technology for virtually free energy, these technologies have been deliberately suppressed. This suppression of technology has not been made to keep secrets from society as we know it but instead is part of a deliberate effort to strategically hide the planet Earth's true technological ability from these malevolent interdimensional entities.

9) The Universe is teaming with life, physical and non-corporal, organic beings, super human intelligence, and weird bands of light that swim in space that are conscious. This life exists everywhere, all around us and in space and on other planets. This life is limitless and has been monitored in space and otherwise for decades. None of this has, up until now, been made known to the public, including but not limited to the vast information collected by astronomical observatories worldwide. The United States Government has identified many types of entities and beings; the ones they are concerned with are malevolent.

10) These interdimensional entities are referred to by our scientists and those involved in the phenomenon as "The Others". The entities we know as "The Greys" are the most interested in the planet Earth and are referred to by those involved in the phenomenon as "The Bugs".

11) These malevolent entities feed on "negative psychological energy". They have existed in their presence on Earth for thousands of years and the rise and fall of civilizations have been directly correlated with humanities exposure and

knowledge of their presence. The societies of Easter Island, the Incans, the Mayans, and Atlantis are examples of civilizations that have disappeared as result of their lack of cooperation with these alien entities.

12) There is an international deep state power struggle going on regarding the disclosure of this interdimensional reality to the public. There is a reason that China has tripled its military budget over the past few years. China, France, Germany, Iran, North Korea, the United States as well as Russia are all working together at a deep state level. Nothing the public sees on the news is as it appears.

10

Acknowledged: The Email

Complete Email Transcript from "The Scientist" as read by Tom Delonge:

"Would the link of aliens creating man then creating God to keep us in our place be something worth keeping secret? I think so. We're talking about the biggest institutions on the planet and the world's major religions.

It's bigger than just the big bad US government and going back to the Greeks and including Russians and Germans make it sufficiently global across centuries. Maybe evidence of disappeared ancient cultures, Easter Island, the Mya, the Inca that's evidence of what happened for those that did not obey thus encouraging the secret to be kept.

Could the story evolve from how different groups of men exploited this technology to see how this entire secret is uncovered, rewriting world history, and shattering many of our most highly regarded worldly institutions; except this time when they come to wipe us out like the other ones we are actually ready for them and that readiness is another example of why things have been kept quiet for so long and it has been a strange international partnership indeed."

Acknowledged: Deaths of Investigators

There have been countless mysterious and suspicious deaths among UFO investigators. In 1971, the well-known author and researcher Otto Binder wrote an article for Saga magazine's Special UFO Report titled "Liquidation of the UFO Investigators:' Binder had researched the deaths of "no less than 137 flying saucer researchers, writers, scientists, and witnesses' who had died in the previous 10 years, "many under the most mysterious circumstances."

The late astronomer Dr. M.K. Jessup was the first to reveal details of the Philadelphia Experiment; he died a few months later.

No one has shaken things up more than Phil Schneider who revealed deep underground bases and the Dulce wars to the world. Schneider died January 17, 1996, reportedly strangled by a catheter found wrapped around his neck. Dr. James McDonald tried to convince Congress to consider the UFO situation. He died after shooting himself a short while later.

If Schneider is telling the truth, he obviously broke the code of imposed silence to which all major black-budget personnel are subjected. The penalty for that misstep is presumably termination. Schneider in fact maintained that numerous previous attempts had been made on his life, including the removal of lug nuts from one of the front wheels of his automobile. He had stated publicly he was a marked man and did not expect to live long. Some of Schneider's more major accusations are worthy of attention:

(1) The American government concluded a treaty with "grey" aliens in 1954. This cooperation pack is called the Grenada Treaty.

(2) The space shuttle has been shuttling in special metals. A vacuum atmosphere is needed for the rending of these special alloys, thus the push for a large space station.

(3) Much of our stealth aircraft technology was developed by back-engineering crashed ET craft.

(4) AIDS was a population control virus invented by the National Ordinance Laboratory, Chicago, Illinois.

(5) Unbeknownst to just about everyone, our government has an earthquake device: The Kobe quake had no pulse wave; the 1989 San Francisco quake had no pulse wave.

(6) The World Trade Center bomb blast and the Oklahoma City blast were achieved using small nuclear devices. The melting and pitting of the concrete and the extrusion of metal supporting rods indicated this.

Finally, Phil Schneider lamented that the democracy he loved no longer existed. He believed 11 of his best friends had been murdered in the last 22 years, eight of whom had been officially disposed of as suicides.

Ivan T. Sanderson passed away unexpectedly. He was head of a major UFO and paranormal group

Ron Rummel, ex-air force intelligence agent and publisher of the Alien Digest, on August 6, 1993. Rummel allegedly shot himself in the mouth with a pistol. Friends say, however, that no blood was found on the pistol barrel and the handle of the weapon was free of fingerprints.

Ron Johnson, MUFON's Deputy Director of Investigations died quickly and amid very strange circumstances. During a slide show, several people sitting close to him heard a gasp. When the lights were turned back on, Johnson was slumped over in his chair, his face purple, blood oozing from his nose.

Although advanced in years, there are some who believe that Dr. Hynek's death was because of "strange circumstances," due to the high number of researchers who have died of brain tumors or cancer.

Ann Livingston died in early 1994 of a fast-form of ovarian cancer. Livingston made her living as an accountant, but she was also a MUFON investigator and had in fact, published an article entitled "Electronic Harassment and Alien Abductions".

Danny Casolaro, an investigative reporter considering the theft of Project Promise software, a program capable of tracking down anyone anywhere in the world, died in 1991, a reported suicide. Casolaro was also investigating Pine Gap, Area 51 and governmental bioengineering. Mae Bussell, a gutsy, investigative radio host died of a fast-acting cancer just like Ann Livingston and Karla Turner. Bussell was acutely interested in Ufology. Deck Slayton, the astronaut, was purportedly ready to talk about his UFO experiences, but cancer also intervened.

Brian Lynch, young psychic and contactee, died in 1985, purportedly of a drug overdose. According to Lynch's sister, Geraldine, Brian was approached approximately a year before his death by an intelligence operative working for an Austin, Texas, PSI-tech company. Geraldine said they told Brian they were experimenting on psychic warfare techniques. After his death, a note in his personal effects was found with the words "Five million from Pentagon for Project Scanate."

Captain Don Elkin, Eastern Airlines pilot, committed suicide. He had been investigating the UFO coverup for over 10 years. Certainly, nothing is stranger, and breeds speculation more quickly, than the 30 deaths associated with SDI (Star Wars) research at Marconi Ltd. in England between approximately 1985-1988.

Roger Hill, a designer at Marconi Defense Systems, allegedly commits suicide with a shotgun, March 1985. Jonathan Walsh, a digital communications expert employed by GEC, Marconi's parent firm, falls from his hotel room, November 1985, after expressing fear for his life.

Ashad Sharif, another Marconi scientist, reportedly tied a rope around his neck, and then to a tree, in October 1986, got behind the wheel of his car and stepped on the gas with predictable results. In March of 1988, Trevor Knight, also associated with Marconi, died of carbon monoxide poisoning in his car.

Peter Ferry, marketing director of the firm, was found shocked to death with electrical leads in his mouth.

Also during the same month of the same year, Alistair Beckham was found shocked to death with electric leads attached to his body and his mouth stuffed with a handkerchief. He was an engineer with the allied firm of

Plessey Defense Systems. And, finally, Andrew Hall was found dead in September of 1988 of carbon monoxide poisoning. Undoubtedly the most intriguing deaths in Ufology were those of Dorothy Kilgallen, M.K. Jessup and Dr. James McDonald; the former an alleged accident, the latter two purported suicides.

Frank Edwards, the noted news commentator, died of an alleged heart attack on June 24, 1967, on the 20th anniversary of the Kenneth Arnold sighting. Was that coincidence? Probably not. Several other prominent Ufologists died the same day, Arthur Bryant, the contactee, Richard Church, chairman of CIGIUFO and the space writer, Willie Ley. The circumstances surrounding the death of Edwards, who like James McDonald was pushing for meaningful Congressional subcommittee meetings, raise huge questions. It so happens that a "World UFO Conference" was being held in New York City at the Commodore hotel on that very day in June, chaired by UFO publisher and author Gray Barker. Barker stated publicly that he had received two letters and a telephone call threatening that Frank Edwards, who was not in attendance, would not be alive by the conference's end.

The annals of Ufology are frighteningly filled with the deaths of Ufologists from unusual cancers, heart attacks, questionable suicides and all manner of strange happenings. Did former Secretary of Defense James Forrestal really commit suicide as purported by jumping out a hotel window at about the time saucers may have been crashing down in the southwestern desert? Was UFO writer Damon Runyon, Jr.'s suicidal plunge off a Washington D.C. bridge in 1988 really an act of will? What really happened to Dr. B. Noel Opan who, in 1959, after an alleged visit by MIBs, disappeared, as did Edgar Jarrold, the Australian UFOlogist, in 1960.

How do we explain the rash of heart attacks that took so many: Frank Edwards, Rep. Rouse, author H. T. Wilkins, Henry E Kock, publicity director of the Universal Research Society of America, author Frank Scully and contactee George Adamski?

Vanessa Bates, who is the mother of Max Spiers, received a text message from her son days before he died which said 'If anything happens to me, investigate ', and then he died after throwing up two liters of black liquid. Max Spiers, UFO investigator, was found dead in Poland and it was ruled that he died from natural causes despite no post-mortem examination being carried out.

12

Acknowledged: Bill Cooper

Milton "Bill" William Cooper, served in the USAF Strategic Air Command and was a First-Class Petty Officer, QM1, E-6, Naval Intelligence. He was an American conspiracy theorist, radio broadcaster, and author best known for his 1991 book *Behold a Pale Horse*, in which he warned of multiple global conspiracies, some involving extraterrestrial aliens. Cooper also described HIV/AIDS as a man-made disease used to target blacks, Hispanics, and homosexuals, and that a cure was made before it was implemented

In July 1998, he was charged with tax evasion and named a "major fugitive" by the United States Marshals Service. On November 5, 2001, he was fatally shot by Apache County sheriff's officers.

Speech by Cooper delivered November 17, 1989, Los Angeles, California

"For those of you who don't know who I am, I was raised in a military family. My family, my ancestors, since they came to this country, have been government people. We have served in the military, we have been patriots, we have fought in all the wars, we care about this country and believe in the constitution of the United States. We know, as many people don't know, that the Constitution of the United States of America is the United States of America! And that's why we've always been ready to do the things needed to preserve and protect it.

When I left home, I went into the Air Force, the Strategic Air Command. As a child, I'd heard stories from my father and pilots, other pilots, my father was a pilot, about Foo Fighters, UFOs, strange craft that were not made on this Earth. And as a kid, you hear that in passing, and it's neat, and you giggle about it, and you go out and play 'Space Man,' and you forget it.

When I was in the Air Force I met men, who had participated in alien crashed-craft recoveries. Now this intrigued me, it interested me, but it was usually after quite a few bottles of beer that these stories would come out, and sometimes the next morning I couldn't remember what the heck the guy said.

When I left the Air Force I went into the Navy, and this is where everything began to happen for me. I had originally intended to just go from service to service and do something that very few people have ever done before. I was a very adventurous, very crazy young man, and I thought that that would be a   pretty exciting life.

I volunteered for submarines, and while on the submarine USS Tyroot, SS-416, on a transit between the Portland Seattle area and Pearl Harbor, which was our home port; the Pearl Harbor sub base, as the port lookout I saw a craft, saucer shaped, the size of a Midway class carrier, aircraft carrier, for those of you who don't know how big that is; it's huge, come up out of the water approximately two and a half nautical miles off the port bow, which is about 45 degrees to the left of the pointy end of the submarine. It tumbled slowly on its own axis, and went up into the clouds. It appeared to be moving slowly to me at a distance of two and a half nautical miles, but in reality, it was moving pretty fast because it came up out of the water, did a few tumbles, and it was gone!

I then reported it to the officer of the deck. I didn't tell him what it was that I saw because my Daddy didn't raise no fools and in case nobody else saw it I didn't want to be the only looney on board the ship. So, I asked the officer of the deck to help me cover that area, and he did, which is common for officers and lookouts to help each other while on bridge watch because they all hang together if something bad happens.

After a few seconds of watching, the same craft, or another craft exactly   like it, came down out of the clouds, tumbled again on its own axis, and went into the water. Ensign Ball, who was the officer of the deck, was literally shocked! What could I say? Seaman Dejeralimo, who was the starboard lookout, had also witnessed this, and Ensign Ball called the captain to the bridge who was followed by the chief quartermaster who brought a 35MM camera, and we watched for between seven and 10 minutes the same craft, or different craft that looked exactly alike, enter and leave the water. It was an incredible show. I don't know if they knew we were there, or if they even cared, but the craft did not glow, they were metal, they were machines without a doubt, they were obviously intelligently guided, they were huge, and having been in the Air Force and the Navy and knowing what it takes, I knew without a doubt, and know it today, that that machine was not made on the face of this earth. Because there's nothing that man can make, that can fly through the air at a speed like that, tumble on its own axis, and enter the water and effectively fly beneath the sea.

If you've ever been aboard an airplane and then gone aboard a submarine, I know there's probably some of you in this room who have visited a submarine at one time or another, you can readily see just without even any of the technicalities involved how difficult such a thing would be to do. Where would it be built, that size? It was absolutely incredible. It changed my life because then all the stories that I'd heard all my life I knew were true, and I began seeing the world in a different light.

It wasn't long after that I was trained by Naval security in intelligence. I was sent to Vietnam. I was assigned as a patrol boat captain, first in DaNang harbor, given a crew, given a multi-million-dollar patrol boat. My job was to gather intelligence from the people who lived around the harbor and the fishermen who transited the harbor, and maintain the safety and security of the harbor and the shipping.

After about five months I was sent up North to the DMZ, to a place called Qua Vieaf, on the Tacan river. Our base camp was at the river mouth. We were only three miles south of the North Vietnamese border and our job was to patrol the Tacan river from the river mouth to Dang Ha, and then up the Quang Tree cutoff to Quang Tree city, again to get to know the people on the bank, gather intelligence, and to patrol every night and maintain the safety and security of the river and the river traffic.

It was while there that I discovered that there was a tremendous amount of UFO and alien activity in Vietnam. It was always reported in official messages as 'enemy helicopters.' Now, any of you who know anything about the Vietnam war know that the North Vietnamese did not have any helicopters, especially after our first couple of air raids into North Vietnam. Even if they had they would not have been so foolish as to bring them over the DMZ because that would have insured their demise.

Our troops were fired on occasionally by these 'enemy helicopters,' enemy troops were fired on occasionally by these 'enemy helicopters,' and occasionally people would disappear. And on one instance that I know for sure at least one entire village disappeared one night because of alien activity.

The reason they used the term 'enemy helicopters' in messages and dispatches was that in Vietnam you could be overrun at any time, no matter where you were. They did not bring crypto encoding equipment into Vietnam, I'm talking about the machinery. What we did is we had crypto tables, and once we every 24 hours those codes would be no good. So that's what we used. We also, because of the inability to use crypto transmitting equipment, had to devise code words such as 'enemy helicopters.'

When I left Vietnam I was eventually attached to the headquarters staff of the Commander in Chief of the United States Pacific Fleet at Macalappa, Hawaii, which is a little hill overlooking Pearl Harbor, it's a beautiful white building up there, and I was specifically attached to the Intelligence Briefing Team of the Commander in Chief of the United States Pacific Fleet.

It was during this tour of duty that, in the course of my duties, documents were placed in my hands that were so unbelievable and so incredible that it took me quite a while to adjust to the fact that what I was seeing was real. Now for those of you who don't understand how I could come to see this information, let me give you a little short course in security clearance and the need to know and how you get to see classified information if you're in the military or in the government, it doesn't matter which, the rules are the same.

Number one, you need a security clearance, and you've got to have clearance at the level that the information you want to see is classified at. In this instance it was classified 'Top Secret, Magic, Restricted Information,' which I came to find out later is the highest security classification in the Nation. To get that type of clearance, all you have to have is a Federal Bureau of Investigation background check, which takes about six months and they send federal agents to your home, to your old schools, to all your teachers, to your friends, to everybody you put down on your security clearance forms, to all your old addresses, your neighbors, everybody that you've worked for, and it's embarrassing because they don't tell them what they're checking on. They just show them their identification and start asking questions and that's when you find out who's your friend and who's not, because a lot of people get scared and think, 'Bill just robbed a bank and I'm not talking to him anymore.'

Now once you get that it's called a 'B.I.' and for those of you who have received a copy of my service record look on the first page, the DD-214 where it says 'Security Clearance,' you will see the term 'B.I.' That's a 'Bureau of Investigation' clearance. Now at that point, you have the clearance for everything including Top Secret and above. What determines what you get to see is your need to know, and the job that you have determines what your need to know is.

I was assigned to the Intelligence Briefing Team of the Commander in Chief of the United States Pacific Fleet, who had to know everything concerning his area of operations which was one half of the Earth's surface; the

Indian ocean, the Pacific ocean, and all the land masses in between. Believe it or not, if we go to war, if we ever go to war, it's the United States Navy that strikes the first blow and attempts to keep the enemy at bay while we can get ourselves together, at least historically. Nuclear weapons have kind of done away with that concept, but military commanders like to talk about it anyway.

Because of this, and you have no conception of the amount of material and information that an area commander has to know; it's unbelievable, and he has to keep track of this, he has to keep on top of it. He has to know what's happening; he has to make the right decisions. Because it's almost humanly impossible for anyone to do that, they have what's called a briefing team, and it's our job to make sure that he has the correct information, all the time, on a 24-hour basis. And every morning, between 8 and 9 a.m., we would give a briefing which covered everything that happened in the previous 24 hours, and everything scheduled to happen in the next 24 hours, and all the pertinent intelligence reports that we had received since the last briefing that he needed to know and that his staff members needed to know. Occasionally we would get messages marked 'Top Secret, Magic, Restricted Information,' and it would be coded in such a way that all you had were answers to questions which you didn't know what the questions were so you really didn't know what the message was all about.

But eventually I found myself in possession, holding two documents; one called 'Project Grudge,' another one called 'Operation Majority.' Project Grudge contained the history of alien involvement since around 1936, and it began talking about Germany's involvement with a crashed disk that they had recovered in 1936 and were attempting to duplicate the technology. (Die Glocke) They were not successful despite what all these Nazi hunters want to tell you. If they had been successful, we would not have won the war, because you cannot beat those weapons! You cannot out fly those craft, you can't even think about it with conventional aircraft. If Germany had been successful, we would now have a German flag up in front of this podium.

They did make some headway. When we went into Punta Mundy we captured documents, we got some scientists, we got some hardware. The Russians also got some documents, some scientists, and some hardware. It wasn't until 1947 that we were able to capture a craft, ral together but it was everything. And that occurred near the city of Roswell, New Mexico. There were dead aliens recovered from the craft. In Project Grudge I saw photographs of these dead aliens, of the craft; I saw photographs of live aliens; I saw photographs of autopsies, internal organs; I saw photographs of the alien designated 'E.B.', which was held in captivity from 1949 until June 2, 1952, when he died. I saw the history of what they had been able to at that time put together, from incidents in the 1800s, which involved aliens and their craft.

I saw the names of projects. I saw a project that was to fly recovered alien craft that had been recovered intact and undamaged, and some of them were recovered intact and undamaged, and how that happened I have no idea. It was called 'Project Redlight,' and first was conducted from the Tonopah test range in the Nevada test site and then was moved to a specially built area, ordered built by president Eisenhower, called 'Area-51,' code named 'Dreamland,' in the Groom dry lake area of the Nevada test site, by secret executive order. It doesn't exist officially, if you ask anyone, or if you write letters to the government they will tell you it doesn't exist. However if you go out there at several places and see it, fly outside the boundaries and look down and see it, you know it's there, but according to the government it doesn't exist.

The project to fly, test fly these craft, was ongoing until sometime in 1962 when a craft blew up not far from the test sight, in the air, and the explosion was seen over a three-state area. The pilots were killed, they had no idea what had happened or why the craft blew up, but they put Project Red Light on hold until a later date when the aliens supplied us with three craft and personnel to help us learn how to fly these craft. That project is ongoing, and we now have not only alien craft that we are flying, we have craft we have built, using the captured technology, and some of the UFOs that people report seeing in the United States, and maybe even elsewhere, are flown by United States personnel.

That may come as a shock to you. We have technology way beyond the limits of what we have been told. A lot of our development technologically, since the end of

World War II, has been due to the exchange of technology which occurs in the area called 'Area-51' on a regular basis, ongoing.

When James Oberth, Professor Oberth retired, many of you don't know who he is ... not too many space people in here. Professor Oberth was probably one of the greatest rocket scientists and space commentators that ever lived. When he retired, the government gave him a special award, there was a press conference, all kinds of ceremony, and when he got up to speak he said, 'Gentlemen,' and I quote Professor Oberth, he said, 'Gentlemen, we cannot take credit for all the technological developments that we have had in the last decade. We have had help,' and that's where he stopped.

One of the reporters raised his hand and said, 'Professor Oberth, can you tell us what other country helped us?' "He said, 'It was those little guys from out in space,' and then he got down and would not comment any further. Now this occurred in 1959. I can go on and on, but time doesn't allow it.

I will tell you ladies and gentlemen that there are all kinds of things going on all the time, we are making rapid progress in exposing this. Since I have begun talking, people have been coming out of the woodwork at a rapid rate, who know and have pieces of this puzzle, and are helping us to put it together, because I don't have all the answers. I saw an awful lot of material, I have remembered an awful lot of it, I have probably, in my remembering, made some mistakes, and I guarantee you they're minor ones, if I have.

We have just recently, for those of you who didn't believe that the Jason Society of the Jason Scholars, the secret group, existed, we now have a letter from the Pentagon, with 51 names of the Jason Scholars, an admission from the Pentagon that they hold the highest security clearances in the nation, an admission from the Pentagon that they hold the protocol rank of Rear Admiral, and are treated as such on any military installation or in any government office. There are six Nobel Prize winners on that list, there are the elite of the elite of the scientific world, they are the only ones who really know the truth about the technology today and about the real science of physics, because the one that we're being taught all the time ... If you send your kids to college to learn physics you're wasting your money because they're teaching them stuff that doesn't work, it's not true, it's not real. Gravity is not what we think it is. There is a Unified Theory! We already know what it is; it's what makes these craft work. It's absolutely incredible what's going on.

Now, if you want to see what's happening right now, keep watching your movies, keep watching your television commercials, your alien programs on television, read Whitley Strieber's Majestic, which is a part of the contingency plan called 'Majestic' to test the reaction of the population to the presence of aliens on the Earth. I have just finished my study of Whitley Strieber's book Majestic, and I'm going to tell you right now that most of the documents in there, that he says are fiction, are real documents that came right out of Project Grudge. It is part of the government's campaign to leak information out in ways that they can always deny that it's real.

There's only one thing wrong with the information in that book, the stories of the characters in there I know nothing about. What I'm talking about are the supposed government documents that he has in that book. I'm telling you tonight they're real. Those are some of the same documents that I saw in Project Grudge back between 1970 and 1973, and where we have wondered before, now we know that Whitley Strieber is working for the government. We had a suspicion anyway because in the front of his book he states that he got information and was helped by the research team of Moore, Shanderey, and Friedman. William Moore has publicly admitted on July 1 that he is an agent of the United States Government, and we know that the others are too.

This is going to come out, and the reason they're doing it the way they're doing it is they know eventually you're going to find out that it's all true and real. They're desensitizing you so that you're not shocked, so that there's no collapse of society as we know it, so that the religious structure doesn't fall to pieces, so that the stock market doesn't go crazy, because these were their original fears. Now, there's nothing we can do about the last one because it's already happened, there will be a segment of the population that worships the aliens, even though they're no different than us; they're just from somewhere else, and they may look a little different. They are not gods. But there are already people worshiping the aliens and they predicted this would happen when they slapped the secret stamp all over all this stuff.

You know, there's really nothing wrong with what's been happening except No. 1, when they decided to keep it secret they needed to finance it, they couldn't tell the public, so they couldn't tell Congress. They decided to finance it with the sale, importation and sale, of drugs. Now in the documents that I read, in Operation Majority, it specifically stated that when George Bush was the president and CEO of Zapata Oil, he, in conjunction with the CIA, organized the first large-scale drug importation into this country from South and Central America by fishing boat, to the offshore oil platforms of Zapata Oil, and then from there into the beach, thus bypassing all Customs inspections and law enforcement inspections of any kind. They are still bringing in drugs, to a limited extent, in this manner. Another manner is by CIA contract aircraft which, one of their bases of landing is Homestead Air Force Base in Florida. We have affidavits from air controllers who have vectored the planes in, who have made sure that they're not interfered with in any way. We have affidavits from personnel at Homestead Air Force Base who say the planes have been met by Jeb Bush, who is George Bush's son. We have affidavits from people who work in the Gulf of Mexico, in the offshore oil business, that yes indeed, the drugs are coming in, at least some of them, from the offshore oil platforms.

They killed President Kennedy and during the workshop, for those of you haven't seen the tape, I will show you, on the tape, who shot the president and why. Between '70 and '73, in 'Operation Majority' it stated verbatim that President Kennedy ordered MJ-12 to cease the importation and sale of drugs to the American people, that he ordered them to implement a plan to reveal the presence of aliens to the American people within the following year.

His assassination was ordered by the policy committee of the Bilderbergers. MJ-12 implemented the plan and carried it out in Dallas. It involved agents of the CIA, Division-5 of the FBI, the Secret Service, and the Office of Naval Intelligence. President Kennedy was killed by the driver of his car, his name was William Greer, he used a recoilless, electrically operated, gas-powered assassination pistol that was specially built by the CIA to assassinate people at close range. It fired an explosive pellet which injected a large amount of shell fish poison into the brain, and that is why, in the documents, it stated that President Kennedy's brain was removed.

If you've studied the case, you will find that indeed his brain disappeared. The reason for that is so that they would not find the particles of the exploding pellet or the shellfish poison in his brain which would have proved conclusively that Lee Harvey Oswald was not the assassin. In fact, Lee Harvey Oswald never fired a shot, he was the patsy."

13

Acknowledged: Locations of 133 DUMB Sites

The United States and other world powers, prefer to keep their biggest secrets below ground, far from the view of passing satellites and the prying eyes of the public. These locations, some hidden and others not, are spread across the country. Some sources have stated that both the CIA and NSA have relocated their most classified operations to deep underground bases or DUMBs, located under the cover of thousands of feet of earth and eternal darkness.

The U.S. military is sensitive about the location of their military facilities. The Pentagon says there are around 5,000 bases in total with around 600 overseas.

Sources reveal that the boring machines, which some say are nuclear-powered, are USAF designed. These machines are massive, capable of "melting rock." There are different estimates as to how far these machines can tunnel in a 24-hour period. Some researchers posit that it could be up to several miles per day.

While the evidence that we have been visited by extra-terrestrials is overwhelming, at least some of the high-speed discoid aircraft viewed by the public are classified aircraft developed and piloted by USAF personnel. Experts say consumer technology is between three decades and half a century behind the government, the question of whether DUMBs exist or not is moot, their exact purpose is kept from the public. The mystery is what they are used for?

While the exact locations and connecting tunnels of many of these underground facilities are open to speculation, some members of the public have put together maps which depict approximate positions of these classified bases.

Phil Schnieder was a government geologist and Skunkworks engineer who claimed to have worked on many black budget projects. Phil Schneider was involved in the construction of Deep Underground Military Bases (DUMB bases). He alleged that since 1947, deep underground military bases or DUMBs were constructed across the country connected by a series of high-speed rail underground tunnels. It was at an underground facility under Archuleta Mesa on the Colorado-New Mexico border near the town of Dulce, New Mexico location in 1979 that he accidentally stumbled on a cavern filled with hostile, subterranean grey aliens. This spurred the "Dulce Wars" and allegedly left 66 humans dead, and Schnieder badly injured from a secret alien human conflict.

In talks given in 1995, he said that there were 129 active deep military bases in America and two more under construction. He confirmed that there existed a minimum of two underground bases in each state. He also mentioned that there were more than 1,450 DUMB bases worldwide. In 2001, it was reported that this number had risen to 133 active DUMB bases in America. He also revealed that 62 of those 129 DUMB bases were being used as housing facilities for various alien groups that the government had made treaties and agreements with. The rest were being used by humans (military & civilians) for biological, chemical, and mind control development.

Schnieder mentioned in his last lecture in Seattle, Washington (Sep 24, 1995) that he was publishing a book that would expose these government secrets and identify the location of every underground base in America, as he felt the American public were entitled to know what the government was doing with their money and keeping secret from them. When Phil was found murdered in Oregon in early January 1996 with a catheter wrapped around his neck. All his records, alien artifacts, journals, book manuscript, etc. were found missing.

So, as a special tribute to Mr. Schneider, here is a list of 133 known Deep Underground Military Bases (DUMBs) and bases with extensive tunnels in the U.S along with their rumored function. Look at this as a public service.

If things go wrong topside you will now know where to go. Have fun!

ALASKA

1. Brooks Range, Alaska

2. Delta Junction, Alaska 2a. Fort Greeley, Alaska. In the same Delta Junction area.

ARIZONA

3. Fort Huachuca. 31°50′ N 1100 19'48" W, saucer base below, intelligence training above, mind-control incl. too.

4. Gates Pass Base

5. Gila Mountain Area, south of Interstate 8 and approx. 30 East of Yuma, AZ. 290 N 116°W. DUM base.

4. Grand Wash Cliffs, on western edge of the cliffs at the head of Grapevine Wash. Must be reached via hwy 93 and then unpaved roads. DUM base.

6. Green Valley

7. Hualapai Mountains, east side of the mountain range, about 35 mi. SE of Kingman, AZ

8. Rincon Mtn., north side of Rincon Mountain

9. Mt. Lemmon

10. Page, Arizona Tunnels to: Area 51, Nevada Dulce base, New Mexico

11. Safford, near Safford

12. Santa Catalina Mountains – base

13. Arizona (Mountains) (not on map) Function: Genetic work. Multiple levels

14. Luke Air Force Base

15. Sedona, Arizona (also reported detainment camp) Notes: Located under the Enchantment Resort in Boynton Canyon. There have been many reports by people in recent years of "increased military presence and activity" in the area.

16. Wikieup, Arizona Tunnels to: Area 51

17. Yucca (Mtns.), Arizona

ARKANSAS

18. In the vicinity of Hardy and Cherokee Village. 360 19′ N 9°29'W W. Installation purpose not known.

19. Pine Bluff, Ark. area. 34° 13.4′ N 92°01.0'W to 34°30′ N 92° 30'W. saucer base.

CALIFORNIA

20. 29 Palms Marine Base, Identified on military map as airspace area R-2501 N. Saucer base southeast of Ludlow. This is a U.S. alien research, diagnostic facility and rumored UFO base.

21. China Lake, mind control and weapons research

22. Darwin, CA, 4 miles' dues west of Darwin

23. Deep Springs, CA, 37°22' N 117° 59.3' W. saucer base

24. Fort Irwin, CA, 35°20'N 116°8'W W. saucer base

25. Edwards Air Force Base, in the area where Diamond Cr. & the so. fork of the Yuba meet, there are 3 underground UFO bases. 34°8' N 117° 48' W

26. George Air Force Base, CA – saucer base

28. Helendale, Lockheed Underground Facility, 34°44.7' N 1170 18.5' W. Technology for secret projects. There are 3 saucer bases here.

29. Los Angeles, On Hwy 14 towards Edwards A.F.B. after Palmdale, one turns off and after taking several streets to 170th street, north on 170th St. to the Rosamond-1 70th intersection, the second and lower and better maintained dirt road will take you west, and if you take a right going north at the power lines and up to the hilltop you will see the top of an underground NORTHOP facility; Technology for the elite's secret projects. This area was very active in the 1970s. Northrop's facility is near the Tehachapi Mountains. It has been reported to go down 42 levels. It is heavily involved with electronics and hi-tech aerospace research.

30. Mt. Shasta

31. Kern River, CA the hollowed-out mountain next to the hydroelectric facility at the Kern River Project near Bakersfield- reported saucer base

32. Napa Valley- located at Oakville Grade north of Napa, CA. Tunnels also connect the wineries north of Napa, used for white slavery and mind-control. Has a saucer base.

33. Norton Air Force Base- saucer base

34. Quincy, CA, 39° 56.2' N 120° 56.5' W. saucer base

35. Near Palmdale (if one takes Palmdale Blvd. to 240th St. and goes to Ave R-8. One the eastern limit of Ave. R-8 is McDonnell-Douglas's facility called the Uano Facility. One can see it better from the Three Sisters Hills to the south of the facility. Strange shaped disks raise out of the ground on pylons. These attached disks glow and change color. It is involved in hi-tech aerospace technology.

36. Presidio, CA – A FEMA/DOD site for Region IX's regional office

37. San Bernardino, CO, 34° 50' N to 34° 16' N

38. Santa Barbara County – placed in the thick diatomite strata

39. Santa Rosa, 38° 26.4' N 122° 42.9' W, FEMA, Regional center for west coast, what FEMA is doing is mostly kept secret. This is listed as a Communications Antenna Field, but is doing much more.

40. Sierra Nevada Mountains, CA – very deep military base

41. Tehachapi Ranch- 4 saucer bases, Tecachapi Canyon has a new underground base which was finished in Sept. '95. This is the "Unholy 6" base of the Orion's. 35° 20' 118° 40'

42. Trona, CA, 35° 45.5' N 1 77°22.6' W –several miles northwest of Trona, directly under Argus Peak. This DUM sits on China Lake's NWC's land, and may have been built in the '60s.

COLORADO

43. Alamosa, 37° 28.1' N 105°52.2'W W- reported saucer base

44. Book Cliffs, CO, 39° 40' N 108° 0' W near Rifle, CO

45. Boulder, CO–The headquarters for EMC, a type of electromagnetic mind control that is being broadcast to modify the thinking of Americans, and to control slaves.

46. Colorado Springs, NORAD –Canada & U.S., & FEMA, hundreds of people on staff, contains at least 4.5 cubic miles of underground caverns and forty-five underground steel buildings. Many underground chambers are as large as 50, x 100 '. This complex tracks thousands of satellites, missiles, submarines, and UFOs. NORAD also controls many Monarch slaves who have ALEX, JANUS, ALEXUS end time callback programming. NORAD installation has 1278 miles of road underground.

47. Fort Collins- base for Gray aliens

48. Grand Mesa- Orion saucer base

49. Montrore Co.–north of Paradox, in Paradox Valley. The site in Paradox Valley can be reached via Hwy. 90 via Nucla. Page 304 ...

CONNECTICUT

50. North west Connecticut

FLORIDA

51. Massive base- reported saucer base

52. Eglin AFB, 30° 40' N 86° 50' W- Orion saucer base since 1978

GEORGIA

53. Atlanta, GA –FEMA regional center, which is appropriately placed since Atlanta is to become a capital within the NWO redrawing of boundaries. Atlanta is believed to have several underground installations in its area, one to the north at

54. Kennesaw Mtn., Marietta, GA connected to Dobbins AFB and one to the south of Atlanta at Forest Park.

55. Thomasville, 30° 50.2' N 83°58.9' W, FEMA, regional center, they train groups in Search and Destroy missions for when Martial Law is imposed. This is SW Georgia in area of tunnels.

IDAHO

56. Lower Goose Lake area in the general area of Oakley, ID.– Wackenhut of the Illuminati run a "model prison" for the NWO. The worst of the federal prisoners are placed in this underground prison which has 7,100 cells which are filled with about 2,700 federal inmates. A track runs through the middle of the eerie underground facility. Food and showers are on the tracks, and the men are allowed showers once a week. The minimum of lighting is used and the men are beaten senseless if they talk at all. It sits 500'underground.

57. South central Idaho–under the Snake River lava flows between Twin Falls and Idaho Falls.

INDIANA

58. Kokomo, Indiana Function Unknown Notes: for years' people in that area have reported a "hum" that has been so constant that some have been forced to move and it has made many others sick. It seems to come from underground, and "research" has turned up nothing although it was suggested by someone that massive underground tunneling and excavating is going on, using naturally occurring caverns, to make an underground containment and storage facility.

59. Bedford & Lawrence Co. area–continued activity in large old mines indicates a possible government use of the large old quarries.

KANSAS

60. Atchison, KS, the DIPEF underground facility, which the govt. go in an emergency. AT & T maintains an underground facility at Fairview, KS.

61. Kinsley, Tunnels to: Colorado Springs, Colorado; Hutchinson, Kansas; Tulsa Kokoweef Peak, SW California Notes: Gold stored in huge cavern, blasted shut. Known as the "midway city" because it's located halfway between New York and San Francisco.

62. Hutchinson, Kansas Function Unknown Tunnels to: Kinsley, Nebraska. The entrance to the tunnel is underneath Hutchinson Hospital and is huge.

63. Kansas City, Kansas Function Unknown Notes: Entrance near Worlds of Fun

MARYLAND

64. Camp David–just north of the camp is an underground facility important to the intelligence agencies.

65. below Ft. Meade, of the National Security Agency, 10 acres of the most sophisticated supercomputers that can be built, very large complex, massive surveillance of all the world's communications, including all transmissions in the U.S. & world of telephones, telegraph, telex, fax, radio, TV and microwave transmissions.

66. Olney, the facility is between Olney and Laytonsville, on Riggs Rd. off Rt. 108. Another underground facility may also exist in the area, FEMA & possibly NSA, the facility may be 10 levels deep, purpose unknown.

67. Suitland, MD- Classified archives of U.S. Govt. stored here in underground levels. Vaults have extensive amounts of documents which are not indexed. Restricted access with a coded security card. High level intelligence groups operate in the area also.

MASSACHUSETTS

68. Maynard, 42° 26.0' N 71° 27.0' W FEMA, regional center, Wackenhut is here too.

69. Edgewood Arsenal, Maryland Martins AFB, Aberdeen Proving Ground, Maryland

70. Bozeman, Function: Genetics

MICHIGAN

71. Battle Creek, 42° 19.3' N 85° 10.9' W FEMA, regional center, activity secret (not validated)

72. Gwinn, Ml, 46° 16.8'N 87° 26.5' W, near Gwinn is a large underground base which is a key base for sending signals. An AFB is also nearby. Under Lake Superior is an alien base with roads 5,000' deep.

MISSOURI

73. 12 miles south of Lebanon, 36° 02.8' N 115° 24.3' W, near the newly created town of Twin Bridges-reported saucer base

74. In the Bat/Dry/Dead Man/ Howell cluster of caves- reported saucer base

75. St. Francis Mountains, MO (between St. Louis & New Madrid)

NEBRASKA

76. North-central Nebraska

77. Red Willow Co. near McCook, NE

NEVADA

78. Blue Diamond, 36° 02.8'N 115°24.3 W - reported saucer base

79-81. Groom Lake, also known as Dreamland, Area 51, The Area, the Spot, Red Square, Sally Corridor, Watertown Strip. 1150 50'N 37°20W. The CIA is there and Wackenhut Security.

Two large underground facilities close to but separate from Groom Lake are Papoose Range and Cockeyed Ridge (S-4) underground bases. Purpose is the testing of various UFOs and other secret aircraft like the Aurora and Stealth. Many levels have been built t these three complexes, and a 7-mile-long run way (which is 39 miles) has been built over Groom Lake, a dry lake. There is an S-2, an S-4, an S-6, and an S-66 underground installations. S-66 is the most secret and it has 29 levels and is 11, 300' deep.

82. Quartzite Mountain SE of Tonopah, 37° 31 'N 116° 20' W- reported saucer base

83. Tonopah, Airforce, CIA? & ??, deals with secret aircraft

84. Mercury, Nevada Function unknown

NEW HAMPSHIRE

85-86. There may be as many as three underground installations in New Hampshire's hills (according to reports).

NEW JERSEY

87. Picatinny Arsenal, 4o° 38'N 74° 32' W- saucer base, 1/4 cubic mile large & very deep underground.

NEW MEXICO

88. The state of New Mexico and Colorado have been used for the construction of a series of underground bases. (All the rest of the states have too.) The Primary Underground facilities in New Mexico consist of: 3 enormous underground bases in the Dulce, NM area.

89. The White Sands, Alamogordo Area which has 3 underground bases. Datil and Pie Town which have two more underground bases. (Carlsbad Cavern which had underground activity, which is reported discontinued, and another base to east of Carlsbad.).

90. The Los Alamos area underground facility. the Taos area underground facility. The New Mexico area has basically four underground system out. One goes to the Four Corners area and then to Groom Lake (Area 51). One goes north toward Delta, CO and Colorado Springs. The Taos facilities goes north approximately along Interstate 25 and eventually ties in NORAD. The southern bases connect to Texas and Mexico.

The Los Alamos facility dates at least back to 1940. One can only imagine what has been built with 1/2 century of labor on this underground system. Visitors to the deeper levels report humans kept in glass cylinders, plus many other strange things. There are special badges, special uniforms, tube elevators etc. which for lack of time I will not describe.

91. Angel Peak- reported saucer base. Carlsbad Cavern area (now destroyed), 32° 25.0'N 1040 14.0W -old relics of saucer base left.

92-94. Dulce, N.M., 36° 56.0'N 106°59.8'W, South of Dulce, around the Jicarilla Indian Reservation, another facility is east of the Dulce facility several miles. This is run directly by the Army with Airforce help, CIA also conduct experiments at the center; the size of the installation is huge, requiring small shuttle trains and has seven levels according to witnesses. Serves as a UFO base, biological experiments, production center for small-grey drones. Wackenhut provides some of the security on the ground.

95. Kirtland AFB, NM, Sandia National Lab

96. Manzano Mountain, near Albuquerque, known as the Kirtland Munitions Storage Complex, Airforce, 3,000-acre base within the Kirtland AFB/Sandia National Labs complex, guarded by 4 lethal rings of fences, use unknown, suspected UFO base. A new 285,000-sq. ft. bunker is being built near Manzano Base.

97. Pie Town, 34° 17.9'N 1 108°08.7'W, in area near Pie Town, UFO Base.

98. Sandia Mountains NE of Albuquerque -reported saucer base

99. to the north of Taos Pueblo

100. White Sands, 32°22.8'N 106°28.8'W, major hub for research, tied in with Dulce & NORAD, HO for NASA/military shuttle flights, radiation research ctr. and mind control.

NEW YORK

101. Adirondack Mountains (near Elizabethtown)

102. New York Metro area function unknown Tunnels to: Capitol Building, D.C.

103. Plattsburgh (near Canada and St. Albans) AFB, 49°40'N 73°33 W- two saucer bases in this area.

OHIO

104. Wright-Patterson Air Force Base - Dayton, Ohio Function: Air Force Repository. Rumored to house stealth technology and prototype craft

OKLAHOMA

105. Ada, 34°46.4' N 96°40.7W W, underground saucer base, this base does human cloning, and it is FEMA's most sensitive base.

106. Ashland Naval Ammunition Depot, 34°45.9'N 96° 04.3'W, - reported saucer base

OREGON

107. Bull Run, north side of Bull Run Reservoir area near Mt. Hood, and very close to Larch Mtn. and south of Benson St. Park of the Columbia Gorge.

108. Coos Bay area has had three separate but coordinating underground facilities built for UFOs. The facility farthest east, about 20 miles inland in the wilderness near Hwy 42, has been shut down. It is now an old abandoned facility well camouflaged. The coast facility is probably still operational.

109. Klamath Falls, OR–since Sept. '95 this has been a base for a few NWO groups including the Air National Guard, FEMA, CIA, FBI, and MOSAP training base. An underground concentration camp exists here.

110. Crater Lake, Oregon Tunnels: possible to Cave Junction

111. Wimer, Oregon (Ashland Mt. area) Function: Underground Chemical Storage Levels: At least one

PENNSYLVANIA

112. Blue Ridge Summit, near Ft. Ritchie, known as 'Raven Rock" or "Site R", Army, major electronic nerve center, 650 ft. below surface with about 350 staff and over a 716-acre area. possibly connected via tunnel to Camp David. The NOD installation is involved with psychic and satellite control over slaves. This underground complex is to allow the government of the United States to escape a nuclear attack. The enormous complex radiates under Wash. D.C. and connects with many other sites. The walls and ceilings of the tunnels are ceramic tile with fluorescent lighting recessed into the ceilings.

TENNESSEE

113. MILLINGTON, TENNESSEE. Naval Support Activity Mid-South, 21 miles north of Memphis. It is an enormous facility, covering thousands of acres. I have been told that there is a deep underground facility beneath this base.

TEXAS

114. Ft. Hood, TX, 31° 15'N 97° 48' W, home of some Delta Mind-Controlled soldiers and a reported saucer base.

115. Denton, TX, 33° 13.2'N 97° 08.2'W – FEMA, regional center, activity secret

116. Red River Arsenal, TX- reported saucer base

117. Calvert, Texas Function unknown

118. Fort Stockton, Texas Function: Unknown Tunnels to: Carlsbad, New Mexico UTAH

119. Calvert, Texas Function unknown

120. Fort Stockton, Texas Function: Unknown Tunnels to: Carlsbad, New Mexico

UTAH

121. Dugway, Utah Function: Chemical Storage, Radiation storage.

122. Salt Lake City Mormon Caverns Function: Religions archives storage. Levels: Multiple Tunnels to: Delta, Colorado & Riverton, Wyoming

123. In Utah, the Kennecott Copper Company has been connected to the Illuminati and the KKK. These connections have been exposed in other writings by this author. Kennecott's mine (reported to be owned by the World Bank) in the Salt Lake City area is serviced by Union Pacific, which is reported connected to the Mormon Church. The mine is receiving a heavy volume of big trucks after 11 p.m., for instance, in a normal night over 6 dozen large trucks with 2 trailors each rolling into the mine. In other words, it appears that the heavy train & tractor trailor activity indicates something besides mining.

VIRGINIA

124. Blue Mont, Mount Weather base, Federal Preparedness Agency & FEMA, small-city underground, top-secret, staff of several hundred, does secret work for FEMA and contains a complete secret government with the various agencies and cabinet-level ranking administrators that keep their positions for several administrations and help run the United States.

125. Culpepper, 380 28.5 N 77°59.8'W, about 2 miles east of Culpepper off Rt. 3, called Mount Pony, Illuminati–Fed. reserve, 140,000 sq. ft.,

includes a facility for the storage for corpses, monitors all major financial transactions in the U.S. by means of the "Fed Wire", a modern electronic system.

126. Pentagon, Arlington, VA-

127. Warrington Training Ctr. – two sites: one on Rt. 802 and the other on Bear Wallow Road, on Viewtree Mountain. One is Station A the other Station B. Army, purpose unknown.

WASHINGTON

128. Bothell, 47°45.7'N 122°12.2w W, FEMA, regional center, activity unknown

There are armed guards stationed at the gate. It's interesting to note is that this FEMA center was home to a Nike Missile Base during the Cold War. All the locals in the area over the age of 40 are aware of this fact, so I know they have underground facilities. What's odd about this base is that the massive complex sits right in the middle of a residential neighborhood.

Bothell's Nike Hill Home to Regional FEMA Headquarters. "The steep hill west of Bothell's Canyon Park, that 228th Street

SE traverses, is known as Nike Hill. Most probably think it's because it's a grueling run for anyone trying to get into shape.

But the site at the top of the hill, where the headquarters of the Federal Emergency Management Agency Region X sit behind a chain-link fence and manned security gate, was once a Nike missile site during the height of the Cold War. The site was active from 1957 to early 1963, and was eventually decommissioned in 1979 and offered for free to FEMA to set up its regional office.

What looks like an unimposing collection of one-story buildings is in fact a multiple-story underground complex where about 170 people work year-round preparing for and mitigating disasters in Washington, Oregon, Idaho and Alaska. While these states are Region X's priority, staff is on-call to respond to any emergency nationwide."

WASHINGTON, D.C.

129. WHITE HOUSE, 38°53.5'N 77°02.0'W–The secret NOD underground installation which is connected to the intelligence groups like NSA and the CIA as well as many other nefarious groups lays under the White House with tunnels connecting this NOD installation with the House of the Temple. Tunnels to: New York City; Mt. Weather. The Supreme council of the 33° of the Scottish Rite's House of the Temple has a 14' x 25' room in it with 13 chairs where the Illuminati's Grand Druid Council meet. The NOD Deep Underground Installation has numerous levels to it. One eye- witness, went to level 17 (via an elevator) and stated that he believes that deeper levels exist.

WEST VIRGINIA

130. Sugar Grove, the Navy's Strategic Intelligence Services microwave communications.

131. White Sulphur Springs, under the Greenbriar Hotel, a mini-city large enough for 800 people equipped with its own crematorium, if there are any other purposes other than listening to U.S. microwave communication it is unknown by this author.

WYOMING

132. Riverton, Function unknown Tunnels to: Salt Lake, Utah Denver, Colorado.

UTAH

133. In Utah, the Kennecott Copper Company has been connected to the Illuminati and the KKK. These connections have been exposed in other writings by this author. Kennecott's mine (reported to be owned by the World Bank) in the Salt Lake City area is serviced by Union Pacific, which is reported connected to the Mormon Church. The mine is receiving a heavy volume of big trucks after 11 p.m., for instance, in a normal night over 6 dozen large trucks with 2 trailers each rolling into the mine. In other words, it appears that the heavy train & tractor trailer activity indicates something besides mining.

Mysteriously, Phil Schnieder is now dead. However, a man named Thomas Edwin Castello, says he is former Dulce base security officer and that this under-world city is, in fact, a highly secret base operated by humans as well as aliens. We know that until 2009 Thomas lived with his wife Marilyn in Roswell, New Mexico. He attended St. John's University in Canada, graduated in 1967 and is listed as "Lost Alumni". He too seems to have, at least disappeared.

What we know for certain is that people have come forward with these claims. Dr. Paul Bennewitz is an electronics specialist who in the late 1979 began to film, photograph, and electronically intercept what appeared to be extensive UFO and ET activity and communications, traced to the vicinity of the Archuleta Mesa on Jicarilla Apache Reservation land near the town of Dulce. Based on the collected evidence Bennewitz concluded that an underground extraterrestrial base existed near Dulce that played a role in both cattle mutilations and abduction of civilians. So, maybe Schneider and Castello were telling the truth.

14

Acknowledged: JPL & Aleister Crowley

John Whiteside "Jack" Parsons was an American rocket engineer and rocket propulsion researcher, chemist, and Thelemite occultist. Associated with the California Institute of Technology (Caltech), Parsons was one of the principal founders of both the Jet Propulsion Laboratory (JPL) and the Aerojet Engineering Corporation. He invented the first rocket engine to use a stable, composite rocket propellant, and pioneered the advancement of both liquid-fuel and solid-fuel rockets.

What many people don't know is that Parsons converted to Thelema, the English occultist Aleister Crowley's new religious movement in 1941. Alongside his first wife Helen Northrup, Parsons joined the Agape Lodge, the Californian branch of the Thelemite Ordo Templi Orientis (O.T.O.). At Crowley's bidding, he replaced Wilfred Talbot Smith as its leader in 1942 and ran the Lodge from his mansion on Orange Grove Avenue. Parsons was expelled from JPL and Aerojet in 1944 due to the Lodge's infamy and allegedly illicit activities, along with his hazardous workplace conduct.

In 1945 Parsons separated from Helen after having an affair with her sister Sara; when Sara left him for L. Ron Hubbard, he conducted the Babylon Working, a series of rituals designed to invoke the Thelemic goddess Babylon to Earth. He and Hubbard continued the procedure with Marjorie Cameron, whom Parsons married in 1946.

"The [Babalon] Working began in 1945-46, a few months before Crowley's death in 1947, and just prior to the wave of unexplained aerial phenomena now recalled as the 'Great Flying Saucer Flap'... Parsons opened a door and something flew in.

"A Gateway for the Great Old Ones has already been established -- and opened -- by members of the O.T.O. who are in rapport with this entity [Lam, an extra-terrestrial being whom Crowley supposedly contacted while in America in 1919]."

~ **Kenneth Grant**, O.T.O

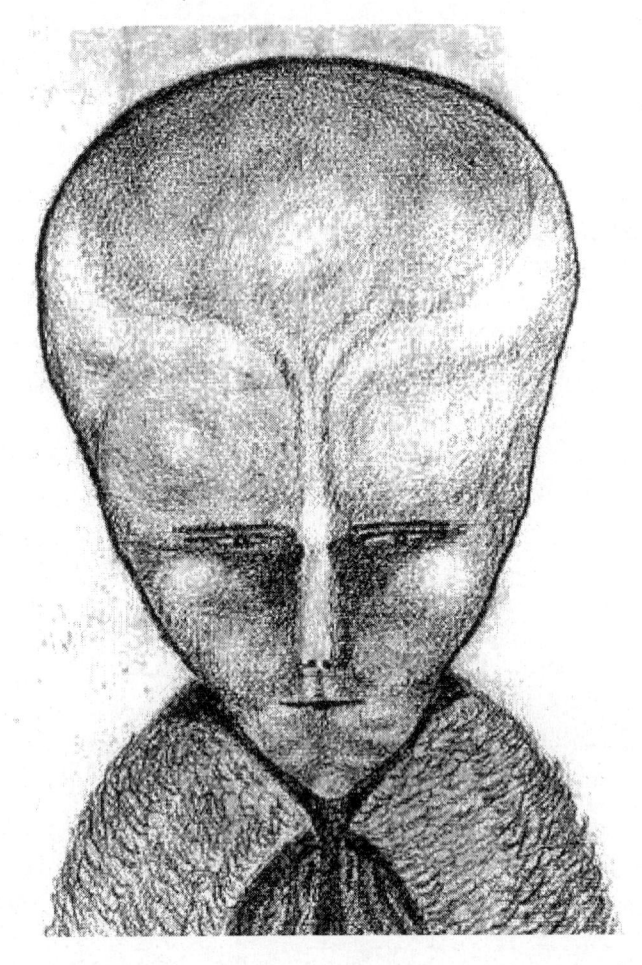

Here's a portrait of "LAM" whom Crowley drew back in 1919. This being, who is considered as belonging to a race rather than a separate individual entity among the

O.T.O and other occultists (most notably the offshoot "Cult of Lam"), bears a striking resemblance to the infamous Grey aliens allegedly working with the secret governments here on Earth.

The theory is that Crowley first made contact back in 1919 through a series of rituals called the Amalantrah Workings. Jack Parsons of jet propulsion science fame, was also a member of the O.T.O and subsequently, he practiced a form of rituals called The Babalon Working which not only reopened the portal Crowley sealed years prior, but ripped open bigger tear in the interdimensional or space time fabric. A tear in which closure was not an option due to inadequate knowledge or careless neglect unlike Crowley. The Babalon Working is patterned after the Amalantrah Working and both involved elaborate use of what they termed "sex magik",

During the Babalon Workings by Parsons on Jan. 14, 1946, strange phenomena was occurring. According to the biography of Ron Hubbard who was a mystical medium during these rituals: 'The light system of the house failed at about 9 pm. Another magician [Hubbard] who had been staying at the house and studying with me, was carrying a candle across the kitchen when he was struck strongly on the right shoulder, and the candle knocked out of his hand. He called me, and we observed a brownish yellow light about seven feet high in the kitchen. I brandished a magical sword and it disappeared. His right arm was paralyzed for the rest of the night.'

The Cult of Lam circulated a manuscript amongst O.T.O initiates called The Lam Statement which revolves around and is dedicated to "regularizing the mode of rapport and constructing a magical formula for establishing communication with Lam.".

According to O.T.O chief Kenneth Grant, Lam is known to be a link between the star systems of Sirius and Andromeda. Lam is the gateway to the Void. Its number, 71, is that of "NoThing", an apparition. Lam, as a Great Old One, whose archetype is recognizable in accounts of UFO occupants. Lam has been invoked to fulfill the work set afoot by Aiwass; as a reflex of Aiwass. Lam as the transmitter to AL of the vibrations of LA via MA, the key to the Aeon of Maat. Lam is the occult energy beaming the vibrations of Maat and may proceed from that future aeon.

What's interesting here is the time correlation between Parsons rituals and when a man by the name of Kenneth A. Arnold made what is the first widely reported UFO sighting of 9 silver disc like craft in Washington state on June 24, 1947. Parsons conducted his rituals from January thru March of 1946. After those rituals, UFO observation was facilitated and UFOs were bursting upon the scene left and right. Of course, the Roswell incident is right up there in the mix as well as George Adamski's observations.

The United States government has discovered and verified the existence of an interdimensional intelligence responsible for not only many races and types of extraterrestrial entities but also paranormal phenomenon like ghosts and demonic poltergeist activity. OK, take a breath. How the hell are you going to explain this to the kids? If you are like me then you realize that our understanding of the world we live in has just fundamentally changed. We are not alone, we never are alone and we never were.

15

Acknowledged: Antarctica

Finally, Scientists believe a massive object that could change our understanding of history is hidden beneath the Antarctic ice. The huge and mysterious "anomaly" is thought to be lurking beneath the frozen wastes of an area called Wilkes Land. The area is 151 miles across and has a minimum depth of about 2,700 feet.

Some researchers believe it is the remains of a truly massive asteroid more than twice the size of the Chicxulub space rock that wiped out the dinosaurs. If this explanation is true, it could mean this killer asteroid caused the Permian-Triassic extinction event, which killed 96 percent of Earth's sea creatures and up to 70 percent of the vertebrate organisms living on land.

However, there are other theories. Since 2016 there has been a lot of speculation that scientists have found evidence of a pre-Adamite civilization of extraterrestrial origin there in the tundra. Speculation began at about the same time as the visit of Russian Orthodox Patriarch of Moscow Kirill III, a visit followed by Secretary of State John Kerry, at the height of the American presidential election. Then, the most recent visit of former Apollo 11 astronaut Buzz Aldrin, who had to be medically evacuated, as his "condition" had "deteriorated." The Aldrin evacuation follows a string of such medical evacuations.

Now, after the Kerry visit, it is being claimed that a Nazi UFO base is visible in images of the Antarctic taken by NASA. In fact, there was a NAZI outpost discovered there in 2016 by Russian scientists. The site, located on the island of Alexandra Land 1,000km from the North Pole 0150 was constructed in 1942, a year after Adolf Hitler invaded Russia. It was codenamed "Schatzgraber" or "Treasure Hunter" by the Germans and was primarily used as a tactical weather station.

Brian, 59, a former retired US Navy petty officer first class and flight engineer in a squadron called Antarctic Development Squadron Six has claimed to have seen the entrance to a secret alien base and UFOs while on duty in the Antarctic. He is said to have seen 20 years of service, and revealed the startling story to American Emmy Award-winning TV producer, investigative journalist, Linda Moulton Howe who claims to have verified his background.

He was said to be stationed there between 1983 to 1997, when he retired, and on several occasions, saw "aerial silver discs" flying over the Transantarctic Mountains. He stated in an interview that there is a top-secret collaboration between humans and aliens, with Antarctica a major research ground for the projects. The large hole was said to be five to ten miles from the South Pole, in the supposed no fly zone.

He also said a group of scientists had gone missing for a week and come back terrified and refusing to speak. Then at a camp near Marie Byrd Land, some dozen scientists disappeared for two weeks and when they re-appeared, Brian's flight crew got the assignment to pick them up. Brian says they would not talk and "their faces looked scared".

He stated, "The only thing we saw going over this camp was a very large hole going into the ice. You could fly one of our LC130 into this thing. Talk among the flight crews was that there is a UFO base at South Pole and some of the crew heard talk from some of the scientists working with and interacting with the scientists at that air sampling camp/large ice hole."

Howe published his redacted DD-214 document and Antarctic Service Medal given to Brian on November 20, 1984 to confirm his credentials. What does this all mean? The UFO enigma is more complex than any one book could ever do encompass. The fact is that you could fill a dozen books with statements and documentation that has been declassified and sits in government databases accessible online. The one thing that is certain is that the reality has been acknowledged at every level of government and private industry short of a formal televised disclosure by a sitting American President. The evidence is overwhelming and, in time, I believe that too will come to pass but until then, enjoy the mystery.

16

Acknowledged: Genesis

In 2016, a group of Hebrew scholars who are part of an effort called "The Chronicle Project", released a new translation of the book of Genesis from the Bible based on new methods of translating ancient Hebrew glyphs. Two chapters of this translation are presented here. Make a special note of references to, "the Originators".

Genesis Chapters 1-2

{1:1} In the beginning, a group of extraterrestrials called the Originators made the heavens and the Earth.

{1:2} And the Earth had existed a long time so they proceeded to develop what was on it. And darkness had come upon the surface of the ocean as the Sun was going breathable atmosphere to be upon the surface of that water.

{1:3} And so the Originators said, "Let there be light." And so, existed that which illuminates.

{1:4} And the Originators saw the Sun which gives light to be good and so, the Originators made distinction between, Sunlight and the darkness.

{1:5} And so, the Originators called the light, day and toward the darkness called night. And so, existed Sunset and then Sunrise of the day "To Unify". Day one.

{1:6} And so the Originators declared, "There shall be sky, separate from the water".

{1:7} And to finish, the Originators took to the sky and they separated the water from the sky and created an atmosphere in the sky. And so, it came to be in this way.

{1:8} And the Originators named the sky "the Locators" or stars. And it became evening and morning, the second day.

{1:9} The Originators declared, "Let the waters from the night of heavy rain pouring down and below it flows toward certain places; rivers, lakes, streams, etc. And they also saw dry land. And so, it came to be in this way.

{1:10} And the Originators called the dry land "Earth" and the waters that gathered around them called, "measures" or seas. And the Originators thus saw it was satisfactory.

{1:11} And the Originators declared, "Let us proceed to sprout the Earth.

{1:12} And things began to grow on the Earth, sprouts of young shoots, those to seed, to sow replicas of themselves. And trees, established to bear fruit, sow seed to make replicas of themselves. And so, the Originators saw this and it was satisfactory.

{1:13} And so, existed Sunset and Sunrise of the day.

{1:14} And so, the Originators declared, "Let there exist that which continues to change, the Moon, amid the sky of the celestials, which can move between day and night. And it shall exist being for creation of tides, congregations, measures and years.

{1:15} And the Sun would continually illuminate the sky and the celestials would help to understand the world better here on Earth. And it came to be in this way.

{1:16} And so, the Originators finished by, pairing a group. The Moon, that which continues to change, could be observed for multiple reasons, understand the Sun that which illuminates, the one that is regarded for continued management of the day. And the Moon shall join the Sunlight, to diminish the night, to continue to manage the understanding of time, along with the stars.

{1:17} And so the Originators changed the orbit of the Moon to join the use of the stars in the sky for understanding time and seasons and for this understanding to spread out upon the Earth.

{1:18} And the Earth's movement created light amid day and amid night in the sky the movement caused an alternation between the light and darkness. And so, the Originators understood it was satisfactory.

{1:19} And so existed Sunset and Sunrise of the day. Day four.

{1:20} And so the Originators declared," Let us divide into separate species everything that lives in the water, all divisions of life therefore to live. And what flies, release upon the Earth and rise upon the face of the celestial sky.

{1:21} And then the Originators created the great sea creatures, and everything with a living soul and the ability to move in the waters and they produced, per their species, and all the flying creatures, per their kind. And the Originators saw that it was good.

{1:22} And they blessed them, saying: "Increase and multiply, and fill the waters of the sea. And let the birds be multiplied above the land."

{1:23} And Sunset came and then Sunrise of day. The fifth day.

{1:24} And so the Originators declared, " Begin to fill the Earth with life. Herd animals and producers of mass offspring. And it came to be in this way.

{1:25} And the Originators made the wild beasts of the Earth per their species, and the cattle, and every animal on the land, per its kind. And the Originators saw that it was good.

{1:26} And so the Originators declared, "Let us use Adam as a guide, to make a copy. This blood being to increase the type of beings. And they shall journey being amid that which swims the sea and that which flies the skies, amid herds, in all the Earth, and amid all the producers of mass offspring to mount the Earth."

{1:27} And so the Originators began to produce a person to join Adam, a female. And the Originators created her in their own image.

{1:28} And the Originators blessed them, and he said, "Increase and multiply, and fill the Earth, subdue it, have dominion over the fish of the sea, the flying creatures of the air, and over every living thing that moves upon the Earth."

{1:29} And the Originators said: "Behold, I have given you every seed-bearing plant upon the Earth, and all the trees that can sow their own kind, to be food for your nourishment.

{1:30} And for all the animals of the land, all the flying things of the air, for everything that moves upon the Earth in which there is a living soul, so that they may have these to eat." And so, it became.

{1:31} And the Originators saw everything that they made and they were very satisfied. And it became evening and morning, the sixth day.

Chapter 2

{2:1} And so the heavens and the Earth, having been terraformed, were completed, with all their adornment and of accomplishments. the Originators admired these

{2:2} And on the seventh day, the Originators fulfilled their work. And on the seventh day they rested from all their work, which they had accomplished. The Creator of the Originators made the Originators to be upon the Earth and he began to prepare the Adam to serve the heavens.

{2:3} And ruler, Adam, was to rise, derived of the Earth and the water which had joined all the surface of the ground.

{2:4} And so the Creator of the Originators fashioned Adam, by joining elements derived of the ground. And so, his body captured a life force to continue to establish memories. And so, Adam existed to have life therefore flow out of him.

{2:5} And so the Creator of the Originators wandered amid the enclosed area that he made to think and Adam joined the established names that he had fashioned

{2:6} And so the Creator of the Originators sprang up all trees from the ground that were delightful to look at and satisfying to eat. And the tree of memories was in the middle of the garden, a special tree of knowledge to both satisfy and fear.

{2:7} And the Originators made the sky and divided the waters that were under the sky, from those that were above the sky. And so, a river came forth to continuously pour out toward that which was set down and join the garden, for navigation, to divide the land, and flow in the four directions.

{2:8} Now the Originators had planted a paradise of enjoyment from the beginning. In it, they placed the man whom the Creator had formed.

{2:9} And so, it became possible to show the location of the gold of the Earth and semi-precious stones to be shown.

{2:10} And a river went forth from the place of enjoyment to irrigate Paradise, which is divided from there into four heads.

{2:11} The name of one is the Phison; it is that which runs through all the land of Hevilath, where gold is born.

{2:12} And so the Creator of the Originators took Adam for a walk and led him to the middle of the garden, to sit down, guard and assist him

{2:13} And so the Creator of the Originators declared to Adam, "You may proceed to consume the fruits of the trees of the garden which are to eat.

{2:14} And that tree of the lasting knowledge which is satisfying and fearful, do not proceed to consume that being from the tree or you will die.

{2:15} And so, the Creator of the Originators declared "It is not satisfactory for Adam to continue to exist alone. To begin to help with this I will create another being.

{2:16} And so Creator of the Originators made of the ground, all living creatures of the field and all to fly the celestials. And Adam named all of those born to live.

{2:17} And so Adam gave permanent names to all the animals. To all those which travels in herds, those which fly the heavens and all living creatures of the field. And Adam had nobody to help

{2:18} And so Creator of the Originators anesthetized Adam so he slept. And so, the Creator took from his body what was needed to create a duplicate and then the Creator closed the wound and it healed.

{2:19} And so Creator of the Originators created a mate to give to Adam. And so, she was admitted to the garden with Adam.

{2:20} And so Adam declared, "She is of my body. She will be called "woman".

{2:21} This joining of man and woman so enables a man to father a child. And this joining with the wife unifies.

{2:22} And so this was fully explained to the two of them, his arrangement.

{2:23} And Adam said: "Now this is bone from my bones, and flesh from my flesh. This one shall be called woman, because she was taken from man."

{2:24} For this reason, a man shall leave behind his father and mother, and he shall cling to his wife; and the two shall be as one flesh.

{2:25} Now they were both naked: Adam, of course, and his wife. And they were not ashamed.

Copyright 2017, All Rights Reserved

Made in the USA
Middletown, DE
27 October 2017